The Collection and Codification of the Quran

Alan Paton

Published by Parkhill Books

Parkhill Books, London

parkhillbooks.com

First Published 2021

Version 1.1

Contents

Tables and Diagrams

Diagrams

Conventions and Abbreviations

Dates

Two dating systems are used; "After *Hijra*", indicated by "AH", the number of Islamic lunar years after Muhammad and his followers migrated from Mecca to Yathrib (now Medina), and "Current Era", indicated by "CE".

The *Hijra* occurred in 622 CE. An Islamic lunar year is 354 or 355 days. ANNEX 4 has an AH-CE conversion table.

Abbreviations

r. concerning a range of dates stands for "ruled"
g. concerning a range of dates stands for "governed"
c. concerning a date stands for "circa", about
d. stands for "died"

Names

The transliteration of Arabic names and words has been kept very simple showing only the Arabic "ayn" (') and "hamza" (') in some cases. The term "ibn" (son of) is written as "b." except when it is part of the short version of the name by which the person is usually known.

Sources in Text

All research papers, studies, and books mentioned or quoted in the text are listed in the Bibliography.

Preface

This book examines Muslim tradition and modern scholarship concerning how the Quran came into existence as written pages between two covers. How this happened and how the text was agreed is not always clear and there are different explanations.

Muslim tradition is a huge field, and it is a formidable challenge to draw out and understand what it has to say about the collection and codification of the Quran, a subject of great importance. The information is sometimes inconsistent or contradictory involving different caliphs and scholars.

Arabian society at the time of the Prophet depended on oral transmission, the word "Quran" means recitation, and Arabic writing was at an early stage of development with fewer symbols, and written words might be read in different ways. Variant readings of the Quran became a concern and traditions refer to a range of differences. It wasn't until the late third century AH that seven canonical readings were firmly established.

The book also explains what we can learn about the early history of the Quran from extant early manuscripts such as the great find at Sanaa in the Yemen and the Birmingham Quran, and the use of radiocarbon dating. Every page had to be hand-written from dictation or copied from another manuscript or written from memory. Writing materials, such as parchment, were scarce and very expensive to produce.

The book is for well informed and interested citizens and students who want to have some depth on key topics, while avoiding the need for extensive prior knowledge. It provides an excellent introduction to scholarly work.

The author is a researcher with many years' experience gathering information from diverse sources and drawing out and presenting the essential elements. The book is a "short read". It is divided into numerous but brief chapters and sections, clearly named in an explanatory style, making it easy to follow and absorb.

Acknowledgements

This book would not be possible but for the works of the dedicated scholars of early Islam and the Quran that the author has drawn on. Their names and works are indicated where appropriate in the Notes and are listed in the Bibliography.

In particular, the author would like to thank the scholars named below who very kindly took the time and trouble of responding to his questions sent by email—from someone they did not know— and making helpful comments.

Daniel Brubaker, Rice University; Yasin Dutton, Oxford Centre for Islamic Studies; Samuel Green, AFES; David S. Powers, Cornell University; Marijn van Putten, Institute for Advanced Study; Gabriel Said Reynolds, University of Notre Dame; Behnam Sadeghi, Oxford University; Gregor Schoeler, University of Basel; Stephen Shoemaker, University of Oregon; Nicolai Sinai, Oxford University; Tommaso Tesei, Duke Kunshan University; Eva Mira Youssef-Grob, University of Zurich

The contents of the book are, of course, entirely the responsibility of the author.

PART 1

COLLECTION

Chapter 1 – Introduction

Our knowledge of how the Prophet's revelations were recorded and gathered together to become the written Quran comes from a host of Muslim traditions.

A Muslim tradition is a report passed word-of-mouth person to person and from one generation to the next. It gives the name of the person who originated the report, the report itself, and the names of the persons in each generation who passed it on.

Traditions were eventually written down, giving the names of the originator and transmitters, and are found in the *sira* (biographies of Muhammad produced after about 125 AH), early Muslim literature about the Quran (mostly after 150 AH), and hadith collections such as al-Bukhari's famous collection produced around 240 AH. [ANNEXES 1-3 give information on these sources.]

No Collection During the Prophet's Lifetime

Numerous traditions say there was no organised writing and collection of the Quran during the Prophet's lifetime. They explain how after the Prophet's death his revelations were gathered together from a wide variety of materials on which pieces of text had been written—from leafless stalks of date-palm trees, from leather strips, from hides, and stones—and from the memories of men, to become the written Quran between two covers.

Traditions also explain why such important material was not put into written and organised form when it first became available. Revelations occurred piecemeal over twenty-three years from the Prophet's first revelation near Mecca in 610 CE to his death in Medina in 632 CE and most likely in the manner of the time circulated orally. While the Prophet was alive there was always the possibility of further revelations and new revelations could and did sometimes abrogate earlier ones. In this state of addition and change, it was not desirable or practical to have or attempt a collection of the text. [1]

Traditions Say a Lot More

The traditions explaining how after the Prophet's death the revelations of the Quran recorded in various ways and in the memories of his contemporaries were all collected together to form a single work and the Quran we have today provides an impressive amount of information and detail. However, the traditions also produce contradictions, a great amount of inconsistency, and pose many questions.

Contradictory traditions identify each of the first four caliphs as the first to organise the collection of the Quran and create a single book. In what appear like attempts to iron out contradictions other traditions have them complementing one another or involving several of them; what was started by Abu Bakr was completed by Umar or what was initiated by Abu Bakr and Umar was completed by Uthman who made a final version.

Some Western scholars suggest that the collection was entirely the work of Uthman, but because he was a member of the Umayyad dynasty which became very unpopular, early Muslims chose to ascribe such an important task as collecting the Quran to his predecessors, Umar and Abu Bakr.

It is puzzling why there should be so much controversy and uncertainty, and what looks like a complicated process, when a good number of the Prophet's Companions had created written collections of the Quran. Why should it have to be put together from a whole range of fragments on assorted materials? Tradition says the Prophet dictated revelations to his scribes telling them the sura in which they should be placed. Why should there be so much concern over some of those who knew it by heart dying in battle, the reason given for the first caliph's collection? [2]

Whatever might have really happened it appears from Muslim tradition it took time, there was a process of some kind, for the Quran to be formally put together, though this did not take long and all was completed less than twenty years after the Prophet's death, in the time of the third caliph, Uthman. [3]

Western scholarship has largely accepted this overview and the Uthman timing though another explanation initiated by Paul Casanova and Alphonse Mingana early in the last century that the Quran was only finally codified—distributed in a single, binding, widely enforced, and accepted form—during the rule of Abd al-Malik, the ninth caliph, some seventy years after the death of the Prophet, has attracted a lot more attention in recent years. [4] This is discussed in Chapter 11.

~~~~

Chapter 2 – The Abu Bakr Collection

The Tradition

According to a widespread tradition found in slightly different versions, the collection of the Quran took place during the rule of the first caliph, Abu Bakr (r. 632–634 CE). It was suggested to the caliph by Umar who was concerned about the number of Quran memorisers and reciters (*qurra*) killed in the battle of Yamama. He feared that large parts of the Quran might be lost. The battle occurred during the Wars of Apostasy (*Ridda* wars) following the Prophet's death probably late in the year 632 CE. Some of those killed might have been the only one to know a particular part.

The full tradition narrated by Zayd b. Thabit, a principal player in what happened, is given in *Sahih* al-Bukhari as follows:

Narrated Zayd b. Thabit: Abu Bakr sent for me owing to the large number of casualties in the battle of Al-Yamama, while Umar was sitting with him. Abu Bakr said (to me), "Umar has come to me and said, 'A great number of Qurra of the Holy Quran were killed on the day of the battle of Al-Yamama, and I am afraid that the casualties among the Qurra of the Quran may increase on other battle-fields whereby a large part of the Quran may be lost. Therefore, I consider it advisable that you (Abu Bakr) should have the Quran collected.' I said, 'How dare I do something which Allah's Messenger did not do?' Umar said, 'By Allah, it is something beneficial'. Umar kept on pressing me for that till Allah opened my chest for that for which He had opened the chest of Umar and I had in that matter, the same opinion as Umar had".

Abu Bakr then said to me (Zayd), "You are a wise young man and we do not have any suspicion about you, and you used to write the Divine Inspiration for Allah's Messenger. So, you should search for the fragmentary scripts of the Quran and collect it (in one Book)".

Zayd further said: By Allah, if Abu Bakr had ordered me to shift a mountain among the mountains from one place to another it would not have been heavier for me than this ordering me to collect the Quran. Then I said (to Umar and Abu Bakr), "How can you do something which Allah's Messenger did not do?" Abu Bakr said, "By Allah, it is something beneficial". Zayd added: So he (Abu Bakr) kept on pressing me for that until Allah opened my chest for that for which He had opened the chests of Abu Bakr and Umar, and I had in that matter, the same opinion as theirs.

So I started compiling the Quran by collecting it from the leafless stalks of the date-palm tree and from the pieces of leather and hides and from the stones, and from the chests of men (who had memorised the Quran).

I found the last verses of Sura al-Tawba: ("Verily there has come unto you an Apostle (Muhammad) from amongst yourselves ....". (9.128-129)) from Khuzaima or Abi Khuzaima and I added to it the rest of the Sura. The manuscripts of the Quran remained with Abu Bakr till Allah took him unto Him. Then it remained with Umar till Allah took him unto Him, and then with Hafsa bint Umar. [al-Bukhari 7191, Book 93, Hadith 53 / Book 89, Hadith 301]*

Al-Bukhari repeats the hadith with slightly different wording. [al-Bukhari 4986, Book 66, Hadith 8 / Book 61, Hadith 509]*

*The references in brackets give the collection in which the tradition is found. Hadith is another term for tradition. Some collections have two organisational forms and there are thus two ways to locate specific traditions. Both are given. The first is used in printed publications and sometimes on the web. The second is widely used on the web.

Historical Facts and Credibility

Yamama Casualties

Several Western scholars have questioned the reason given for this collection. According to the lists of those who were killed at Yamama, very few were likely to have been memorises and reciters of the Quran. Most of those killed were recent converts and not known for their knowledge of the Quran. Following the research he undertook, Friedrich Schwally says *"In the reports on casualties accessible to me there are actually only two men whose knowledge of the Quran is explicitly attested".* [1]

Written Material Existed

The tradition itself says that Zayd b. Thabit who was ordered to take on the collection was a scribe for the Prophet, he *"used to write the Divine Inspiration for Allah's Messenger"* and refers in the main to the collection of written material. This and other traditions indicate that much of the Quran if not all of it existed in written form and knowledge of it was unlikely to depend on the memories of men such as those killed at Yamama. [2] [See Chapter 7, Early Writing and Compilation.]

There is also evidence that a significant number of the Prophet's Companions made their own written copies of his revelations for personal use or teaching the Quran on behalf of the Prophet. These Companion works are discussed in the next chapter.

Lack of Authority

It seems reasonable to expect that a complete copy of the Quran collected by order of the caliph and kept in his possession would acquire high status and be recognised as the authoritative copy of the Quran to which believers should refer. Abu Bakr's rule was short, only two years, but Umar, his successor, who inherited the copy and ruled for ten years (r. 634–644 CE) is recognised as a powerful and successful caliph doing much do expand the world of Islam. Throughout this time there is no mention or evidence for an authoritative caliphal copy of the Quran. [3]

Another surprise is according to the tradition on Umar's death the copy passed to his daughter, Hafsa, instead of to Uthman his successor as caliph. This would indicate that what passed to her was a private possession. An official document would not be bequeathed to a woman, even if she was also a widow of the Prophet, it would go to the succeeding caliph. [4]

Later traditions concerning Uthman's collection of the Quran talk about a copy possessed by Hafsa. [See Chapter 4] There is reason to believe she had a copy but whether it came from Abu Bakr is another matter!

Other Traditions

The tradition given above and its different versions have Umar as the initiator of the idea of collection and Abu Bakr as the one who takes responsibility and implements it.

Another set of traditions has Umar as both the initiator and the implementor with no mention of Abu Bakr. [5] One of these says he died before it was completed. [6]

A third group of traditions has Abu Bakr starting the process of collection and Umar completing it after Abu Bakr's death or that Abu Bakr was the first to collect the Quran on individual sheets (*suhaf*) and Umar the first to put them all together in a single volume (*mushaf*). [7]

Various traditions make claims for each of the first four caliphs to have been the first to collect the Quran. [8]

Some traditions also say there was no effort at all to collect the Quran before Uthman. [9]

Many other traditions contradict the popular accounts as we shall see in Chapter 4 concerning Uthman, the third caliph, and Chapter 7 concerning the view that the Prophet himself was involved in collection.

Partly True?

The above information gives strong ground for believing the accounts of Abu Bakr's collection of the Quran are false.

The reasons given for the creation of such a false tradition are linked to the collection organised by Uthman, the third caliph. On the one hand, it could have been fabricated to bolster the status of Uthman's collection as he is said to have based his version on the copy held by Hafsa. His version was thus based on Abu Bakr's early efforts and thus superior to any rival or pre-Uthman work. [10]

On the other hand, in contrast to the first explanation, the intention could have been to lessen the role of Uthman, who was not a popular caliph, in producing the official text by showing he had used the results of an original collection ordered by Abu Bakr. [11]

Another possibility is that Abu Bakr was simply one of the Companions who collected revelation material and compiled a copy of the Quran for personal use. The existence of such Companion copies is well documented. He would certainly have been in a very good position so close to the prophet to have obtained written records of the Prophet's revelations for himself. [12]

It is also perfectly understandable that Umar, his successor as caliph, would want to have a copy of the Quran. Umar died of wounds before his successor was chosen and in these circumstances it is possible to see why his copy of the Quran, a personal copy, passed to his daughter Hafsa, for safe-keeping.

Other indications of the existence of early comprehensive and pre-Uthman Qurans are the references to missing verses. For example, Umar claimed the verse of stoning was missing. There obviously had to be "complete" works from which such verses could be seen to be missing!

~~~~

Chapter 3 – Companion Codices

What Are They?

Traditions tell us the Prophet made known the words of his revelations not only by teaching them himself but also by selecting others to teach the Quran.

Narrated Masruq: .... I heard Allah's Messenger saying, "Learn the recitation of the Quran from (any of these) four persons: Abdullah b. Mas'ud, [Ibn Mas'ud], Salim the freed slave of Abu Hudhayfa, Ubayy b. Ka'b, and Mu'adh b. Jabal". I do not remember whether he mentioned Ubayy first or Mu'adh. [al-Bukhari 3758. Book 62, Hadith 106 / Vol. 5, Book 57, Hadith 103]

As mentioned in Chapter 1 he also instructed scribes to write down his words. In these circumstances, it is no surprise that those whom he selected to teach and some of his other Companions began written collections of his revelations. This produced what we now call Companion codices. [1]

A codex (plural codices) is a book made up from folded or joined single sheets of parchment, such as vellum, or papyrus, or paper or similar. The term is usually used to describe only hand-written contents. The Arabic for codex is *mushaf* (plural *masahif*)

Though they might have been originally produced for teaching purposes or personal use, after the Prophet's death several of these codices became widely known and authoritative especially in the new parts and settlements of the growing Islamic territory.

All this points to one of the major inconsistencies of the various Abu Bakr traditions concerning the collection of the Quran. The traditions nowhere mention the existence of Companion codices. The existence of such codices would, of course, undermine the reason given for the Abu Bakr collection, that the Quran was being lost by the death in battle of those who had memorised it.

How We Know About Companion Codices

We have no copies of any of these early codices. We know about them only from traditions that mention the collections of

Companions such as Ali, Salim, and Abu Musa, and that give lists of those who made collections though the lists mostly do not agree, from Quran commentaries produced in the 3rd–8th centuries AH, and from the works of later scholars who had access to earlier special works from the period 2nd–4th centuries AH, only one of which has survived, that examined these early codices. [2]

The surviving special work is the *Kitab al-Masahif* (Book of Quran codices) of Ibn Abi Dawud (d. 316 AH) discovered by the famous Western scholar Arthur Jeffery and published in 1937. [Chapter 8 gives more information on early Muslim literature that mentions Companion codices.]

The Most Well-Known

Based on Ibn Abi Dawud's Book of Quran codices and other sources Jeffery identified 15 Companion codices and 13 codices by Successors, the following generation, named by him as Primary codices and Secondary codices, respectively. [3]

The Companion codices most often referred to in the sources are those of Ibn Mas'ud, which was adopted by the people Kufa, in what is now Iraq, Ubayy b. Ka'b, adopted in large parts of Syria, and, Abu Musa, whose codex was adopted by the people of Basra.

Ibn Mas'ud

Ibn Mas'ud (d. 33 AH)(653 CE), was a personal servant of the Prophet. He was one of the *muhajirun* who followed Muhammad from Mecca to Medina. He was highly regarded and was with the Prophet on many important occasions. It is said that he learnt some seventy suras directly from the Prophet and as noted in the tradition from al-Bukhari given above, was chosen by Muhammad to teach the Quran.

When Umar became caliph he appointed Ibn Mas'ud to a government post in Kufa where through his reputation and expertise his codex became the authoritative copy of the Quran.

Various traditions concern his fame and expert knowledge of the Quran. There is even one tradition that says he was present when the angel Gabriel visited Muhammad to revise the contents of the Quran just before the Prophet died. [4]

Another version of the above al-Bukhari tradition emphasises that of those appointed to teach the Quran he is, in fact, mentioned first.

Masruq reported: We used to go to Abdullah b. Amr and talk to him, Ibn Numair said: One day we made a mention of Abdullah b. Mas'ud [Ibn Mas'ud], whereupon he said: You have made mention of a person whom I love more than anything else. I heard Allah's Messenger as saying: Learn [the] Quran from four persons: Ibn Umm Abd [Ibn Mas'ud] he started from him - then Mu'adh b. Jabal and Ubayy b. Ka'b, then Salim the ally of Abu Hudhayfa. [Muslim 2464. Book 44, Hadith 164 / Book 31, Hadith 6024]

He is also recorded himself declaring the extent of his Quranic knowledge.

Narrated Abdullah [Ibn Mas'ud]: .... There is no Sura revealed in Allah's Book but I know at what place it was revealed; and there is no Verse revealed in Allah's Book but I know about whom it was revealed. And if I know that there is somebody who knows Allah's Book better than I, and he is at a place that camels can reach, I would go to him. [al-Bukhari 5002. Book 66, Hadith 24 / Vol. 6, Book 61, Hadith 524]

In another tradition he relates how he even recited the Quran for the Prophet.

Narrated Abdullah [Ibn Mas'ud]: Allah's Messenger said (to me), "Recite the Quran to me". I said, "Shall I recite (it) to you while it has been revealed to you?" He said, "I like to hear it from another person". So I recited Sura al-Nisa (The Women) till I reached the Verse: "How (will it be) then when We bring from each nation a witness, and We bring you (O Muhammad) as a witness against these people". (4.41) Then he said to me, "Stop!" Thereupon I saw his eyes overflowing with tears. [al-Bukhari 5055. Book 66, Hadith 80 / Vol. 6, Book 61, Hadith 575]

Ubayy b. Ka'b

Ubayy b. Ka'b (d. 19/22 AH)(640/643 CE) was a secretary for the Prophet. He is often mentioned in various roles in traditions about the collection of the Quran. For example, some traditions mention the sheets of Ubayy instead of the sheets of Hafsa, and Ubayy plays the part that Zayd b. Thabit is usually assigned.

As for Ibn Mas'ud, various traditions demonstrate his fame for knowledge of the Quran. The Prophet praises him.

Affan b. Muslim informed us ... on the authority of Anas b. Malik, he on the authority of the Prophet, may Allah bless him; he said: The best reader (of the Quran) among my people is Ubayy b. Ka'b. [5]

He is said to have been responsible for remembering important revelations on legal matters, and another tradition has the Prophet reciting a specific passage especially to Ubayy.

Anas b. Malik reported that Allah's Messenger said to Ubayy b. Ka'b: I have been commanded to recite to you the Sura (al-Bayyina) which opens with these words (....). He said: Has he mentioned to you my name? He said: Yes; thereupon he shed tears of joy. [Muslim 799. Book 44, Hadith 173 / Book 31, Hadith 6032]

Umar, when caliph, also names Ubayy as the best Quran reciter (though appears to suggest his version might not be entirely accurate!)

Umar said, Ubayy was the best of us in the recitation (of the Quran) yet we leave some of what he recites. .... [al-Bukhari 5005. Book 66, Hadith 27 / Vol. 6, Book 61, Hadith 527]

Abu Musa

Abu Musa (d. 42 AH or later) (662 CE) was a Companion of Muhammad who converted to Islam in Mecca before the *Hijra*. He later held administrative and military positions under the caliphs Umar and Uthman and was made governor of Basra in 17 AH (638 CE) where his codex became established as the authoritative Quran.

Other Companion Codices

The other codices identified by Jeffery as making up the 15 Companion codices are those of:

Umar (Second caliph)

Ali b. Abi Talib (Fourth caliph, cousin and son-in-law of the
Prophet)
Hafsa bint Umar (Widow of Muhammad)
Aisha bint Abu Bakr (Widow of Muhammad)
Umm Salama (Widow of Muhammad)
Zayd b. Thabit
Abd Allah b. Abbas
Anas b. Malik
Abd Allah b. al-Zubayr
Salim the Client of Abu Hudhayfa (Mentioned by Muhammad as
one from whom to learn the Quran. See hadith above)
Ubayd b. Umayr, and
Ibn Amr b. al-As Ali b.

Various hadiths refer to Companions who collected the Quran
during the Prophet's time, for example:

*Narrated Qatada: I asked Anas b Malik: "Who collected the Quran at
the time of the Prophet?" He replied, "Four, all of whom were from the
Ansar [Those in Medina who gave help to the Prophet]: Ubayy b. Ka'b,
Mu'adh b. Jabal, Zayd b. Thabit and Abu Zayd".*
[al-Bukhari 5003. Book 66, Hadith 25 / Vol. 6, Book 61, Hadith 525]

*Narrated Anas b. Malik: When the Prophet died, none had collected
the Quran but four persons; Abu Ad-Darda, Mu'adh b. Jabal, Zayd b.
Thabit and Abu Zayd. We were the inheritor (of Abu Zayd) as he had no
offspring.* [al-Bukhari 5004. Book 66, Hadith 26 / Vol. 6, Book 61,
Hadith 526]

*Anas is reported to have said: Four persons collected the Quran
during the lifetime of Allah's Messenger and all of them were Ansar:
Mu'adh b. Jabal, Ubayy b. Ka'b, Zayd b. Thabit, Abu Zayd. Qatada said:
Anas, who was Abu Zayd? He said: He was one of my uncles.* [Muslim
2465a. Book 44, Hadith 170 / Book 31, Hadith 6029]

Variants of these traditions mention various other names.

Ali b. Abi Talib
Some traditions say Ali b. Abi Talib (d. 40 AH)(661 CE), cousin
and son-in-law of Muhammad, collected the Quran. One such

tradition has him starting his collection while Muhammad was still alive, and on Muhammad's explicit order, but as the tradition comes from Ali's family it is held in suspicion by non-Shi'a. [6]

Other traditions, both Sunni and Shi'a, say Ali collected together his own copy of the Quran immediately after the Prophet's death and this was the first such compilation of the Quran. [7] It is claimed that Ali's version was also unique in that he placed the suras in the order in which they were revealed [8] and indicated abrogated and abrogating verses. [9]

I have sworn not to put on my cloak [and leave the house] except for the Friday prayers – this until I finish the collection of the Quran. And he did indeed collect it.

Ali saw that the people were in dispute after the death of the Prophet, so he swore that he would not put on his cloak until he collected the Quran. He stayed in his house until he collected the entire Quran. This is the first mushaf in which the Quran was collected. He was able to collect it because it was embedded in his heart. This mushaf remained with the family of Jafar. [10]

It is also argued the tradition saying he refused to leave his house until he completed the collection is a politically motivated fabrication. A rumour spread that Ali did not attend the meeting at which Abu Bakr was appointed the first caliph after Muhammad because he did not wish to swear allegiance to Abu Bakr, and the tradition was created later when it became important to show Ali supported the line of first caliphs; he had a good excuse for not attending the meeting. [11]

How the Codices Compared

Jeffery made an extensive study of the early Islamic literature that mentions Companion codices and discusses their content, and of his discovery, the *Kitab al-Masahif* (Book of Quran codices) of Ibn Abi Dawud. He identified thousands of differences, variants, between codices, and lists and describes them in his work *Materials For The History Of The Text Of The Quran* published in 1937. [12]

The differences between codices are an important subject throwing some light on how the Quran was collected and finally canonised in a standard form. [Chapter 9, Companion Codices Compared, provides further information.]

~~~~

Chapter 4 – Uthman

Whatever really happened during Abu Bakr's caliphate there was, some twenty years later, under the third caliph Uthman (r. 644–656 CE) still the need for a standard Quran and some of the accounts of this second exercise involve what was, in effect, an original collection from scratch.

What Happened Under Uthman

According to tradition, in 651 CE Muslim troops drawn from Syria and Iraq undertook an expedition to Armenia and Azerbaijan and disputes broke out between the different contingents over the correct recitation of the Quran during communal prayers. [1]

This horrified the general Hudhayfa b. al-Yaman and as soon as he could he reported the matter to Uthman saying *"O chief of the Believers! Save this nation before they differ about the Book (Quran) as Jews and the Christians did before"*.

Uthman took council with leading Companions and, according to tradition, borrowed the sheets from Abu Bakr's collection that Hafsa had in her possession. He also appointed a commission consisting of Zayd b. Thabit as the leader, the man who had made the collection under Abu Bakr, and three prominent men from Muhammad's Quraysh tribe of Mecca and instructed them to copy the individual sheets of Hafsa's collection into a codex using the Quraysh dialect.

It is not clear exactly what was done and how long it took. There are accounts that it was much more than a copying exercise. There was consultation in Medina and the collection of original material. The whole Quran was carefully revised, the contents of each sura fixed, what should be included or excluded, and the suras placed in order. The result was a fixed and agreed version of the Quran, at least, in the way Arabic was written at that time.

It lacked markings or signs for vowels and showed only consonants, a form of writing that produces what is known as a *rasm*. There were also not enough signs to cover all the consonants and some signs could stand for one or another consonant. The exact word and how it should be said had to be understood from the context or from memory. [More information on early Arabic writing is given in the next chapter.]

When the work was finished Hafsa's sheets were returned to her. Uthman had a copy of the new codex kept in Medina and copies sent to the main centres of the Islamic world, Kufa, Basra and Damascus with strict orders that all other Quranic material whether in whole copies or fragmentary manuscripts had to be destroyed. [2]

Muslims today unanimously attribute the official text of the Quran to Uthman and in light of this most Western scholars accept that at least in terms of the number and arrangement of the suras the Quran we have goes back to Uthman but Uthman's Quran was not completely fixed, it was not necessarily a *textus receptus ne varietur* (the generally accepted text of a literary work that must not be changed).

The Tradition

The main version of the tradition describes events as follows:

Narrated Anas b. Malik: Hudhayfa b. al-Yaman came to Uthman at the time when the people of Sham [Syria] and the people of Iraq were Waging war to conquer Armenia and Azerbaijan. Hudhayfa was afraid of their (the people of Sham and Iraq) differences in the recitation of the Quran, so he said to Uthman, "O chief of the Believers! Save this nation before they differ about the Book (Quran) as Jews and the Christians did before".

So, Uthman sent a message to Hafsa saying, "Send us the manuscripts [sheets] of the Quran so that we may compile the Quranic materials in perfect copies and return the manuscripts [sheets] to you". Hafsa sent it to Uthman. Uthman then ordered Zayd b. Thabit, Abdullah b. Az Zubair, Sa'id b. Al-As and Abdur Rahman b. Harith b. Hisham to rewrite the manuscripts in perfect copies.

Uthman said to the three Qurayshi men, "In case you disagree with Zayd b. Thabit on any point in the Quran, then write it in the dialect of

Quraysh, the Quran was revealed in their tongue". They did so, and when they had written many copies, Uthman returned the original manuscripts to Hafsa. Uthman sent to every Muslim province one copy of what they had copied, and ordered that all the other Quranic materials, whether written in fragmentary manuscripts or whole copies, be burnt.

Zayd b. Thabit added, "A verse from Sura al-Ahzab was missed by me when we copied the Quran and I used to hear Allah's Messenger reciting it. So, we searched for it and found it with Khuzaima b. Thabit al-Ansari. (That Verse was): 'Among the Believers are men who have been true in their covenant with Allah'. (33.23)" [al-Bukhari 4987, Book 66, Hadith 9 and al-Bukhari 4988, Book 66, Hadith 10 / Book 61, Hadith 510]

Another version appears in *Jami'* al-Tirmidhi

Narrated Al-Zuhri: from Anas who said: Hudhayfa b. Al-Yaman came to Uthman, at the time when the people of Sham and the people of Iraq were waging war to conquer Armenia and Azerbaijan. Hudhayfa saw their (the people of Sham and Iraq) different forms of recitation of the Quran. So he said to Uthman: "O Commander of the Believers! Save this nation before they differ about the Book as the Jews and the Christians did before them".

So, he (Uthman) sent a message to Hafsa (saying): "Send us the manuscripts [sheets] so that we may copy them in the Musahif then we shall return it to you". So, Hafsa sent the manuscripts [sheets] to Uthman. Uthman then sent order for Zayd b. Thabit, Sa'id b. Al-As, Abdur Rahman b. Harith b. Hisham, and Abdullah b. Az Zubair, to copy the manuscripts in the Musahif. Uthman said to the three Quraysh men: "In case you disagree with Zayd b. Thabit on any point in the (recitation dialect of the) Quran, then write it in the dialect of Quraysh for it was in their tongue". So, when they had copied the manuscripts, Uthman sent one Mushaf from those Musahif that they had copied to every province.

Al-Zuhri said: Kharijah b. Zayd [b. Thabit] narrated to me that Zayd b. Thabit said: "I missed an Ayah of Sura al-Ahzab that I heard the Messenger of Allah reciting: 'Among the believers are men who have been true to their covenant with Allah, of them some have fulfilled their obligations, and some of them are still waiting' (33:23) - so I searched for it and found it with Khuzaimah b. Thabit, or Abu Khuzaimah, so I put it in its Sura" .... [al-Tirmidhi, English Reference, Book 44, Hadith 3104]

Questions

Why Quraysh?

Schwally, the famous Western scholar, and others have argued that the Quran is not written in the dialect of the Quraysh. He says the Quran is partly in an artificial literary Arabic language and this view is accepted by most modern Western scholars. This casts a big question over the statement in the tradition that Uthman ordered the newly written copy to be in the Quraysh dialect and the work done by the commission. [3]

Hafsa's Copy and What Exactly Was Done

It is not at all clear exactly what was done; the copying and possible organisation of the already collected Quranic text or something more fundamental. [4] Some of the possibilities are given in further traditions, and by what the nature of Hafsa's copy might indicate. The traditions are discussed in a further section below.

There is an account discovered recently that the caliph Marwan (r. 684–685 CE), while he was governor of Medina, tried to get back from Hafsa the sheets in her possession because he wanted to destroy them. He did not succeed but after Hafsa's death he persuaded her brother to hand them over. He wanted to destroy them because they contained readings that were different from the Uthman version and he feared that this would cause more communal dissension. [5]

This implies that Hafsa's sheets were unlikely to have been the main basis for the Uthman text. She may well have had sheets with some Quranic text especially as she was a widow of Muhammad, but these sheets had no special status. The reference to her in the Uthman collection traditions might have been introduced simply to provide a link to the "first collection" under Abu Bakr.

There is another odd point concerning Hafsa's sheets. Uthman ordered that all copies of the Quran text, complete or fragmentary, other than his standard Quraysh text, should be destroyed. Why then, was her possibly less than perfect copy returned to her? According to the Uthman collection tradition itself, it must have had at least one verse missing, the verse found with Khuzaimah b. Thabit, or Abu Khuzaimah.

The Nature of the Differences

The collection and related traditions give very little information on the nature of the differences that caused the general to take the matter to the caliph and why they were so important. [Chapter 5, and Chapters 8, 9, and 10 of PART 2 give more information on this important subject.]

The Last and Missing Verses

Another puzzle concerns the reference to a missing verse in the main Uthman traditions quoted above. For example:

Zayd b. Thabit added, "A verse from Sura al-Ahzab was missed by me when we copied the Quran and I used to hear Allah's Messenger reciting it. So we searched for it and found it with Khuzaima b. Thabit al-Ansari. (That Verse was): 'Among the Believers are men who have been true in their covenant with Allah'. (33.23)" [al-Bukhari 4987, Book 66, Hadith 9 and al-Bukhari 4988, Book 66, Hadith 10 / Book 61, Hadith 510]

This Uthman collection detail bears a striking resemblance to detail given in the Abu Bakr collection traditions. For example:

So, I started looking for the Quran and collecting it .... till I found the last Verse of Sura al-Tawba (Repentance) with Abi Khuzaima al-Ansari, and I did not find it with anybody other than him. The Verse is: "Verily there has come unto you an Apostle (Muhammad) from amongst yourselves. It grieves him that you should receive any injury or difficulty ...." (9.128-129) [al-Bukhari 4986, Book 66, Hadith 8 / Book 61, Hadith 509]

Is it simply a coincidence that two people with very similar names play such vital roles concerning verses, one nearly missed, and one the last to be found, or is the same person and a story copied and repeated with some differences?

Other Traditions

Reasons for the Uthman Collection

Some traditions give completely different reasons for Uthman's collection and different explanations of how it was carried out. A tradition again involves Hudhayfa and disagreements over which reading to follow and this time covers disagreements between different groups of Iraqis, but there is no mention of a military expedition.

Yazid b. Mu'awiya was in the mosque in the time of al Walid b. Uqba, sitting in a group among whom was Hudhayfa. An official called out, "Those who follow the reading of Abu Musa, go to the corner nearest the Kinda door. Those who follow Abdullah's [Ibn Mas'ud] reading, go to the corner nearest Abdullah's [Ibn Mas'ud] house". Their reading of Q 2.196 did not agree. One group read, "Perform the pilgrimage to God", The others read it "Perform the pilgrimage to the Ka'ba".

Hudhayfa became very angry, his eyes reddened and he rose, parting his qamis at the waist, although in the mosque. This was during the reign of Uthman. Hudhayfa exclaimed, "Will someone go to the Commander of the Faithful, or shall I go myself? This is what happened in the previous dispensations". [6]

Another tradition mentions differences between teachers.

During the reign of Uthman, teachers were teaching this or that reading to their students. When the students met and disagreed about the reading, they reported the differences to their teachers. They would defend their readings, condemning the others as heretical. News of this came to Uthman's ears and he addressed the people, "You who are here around me are disputing as to the Quran and pronouncing it differently. It follows that those who are distant in the various regional centres of Islam are even more widely divided. Companions of Muhammad! act in unison; come together and write out an imam for the Muslims". [7]

Unfortunately, the traditions give no useful information on the exact nature of the differences and how they arose.

No Use of Hafsa's Copy

There is an indirect reference to Companion codices but no mention of existing material from an earlier caliphal collection under Umar or Abu Bakr.

Musab b. Sa'd reports, Uthman addressed the people, "It is now thirteen years since your Prophet left you and you are not unanimous on the Quran. You talk about the reading of Ubayy and the reading of Abdullah [Ibn Mas'ud]. Some even say, 'By God. my reading is right and yours is wrong'. I now summon you all to bring here whatever part of the Book of God you possess". One would come with a parchment or a scrap of leather with a Quran verse on it [....] until there was gathered great store of such. Uthman adjured them one by one, "You heard the Prophet recite this?" They would answer that that was so. .... [8]

Uthman Completed Collection Started by Umar

Another tradition has Uthman simply continuing the work of Umar, his predecessor as caliph, and gathering material from numerous fragmented sources.

Umar decided to collect the Quran. He addressed the people, "Let whoever received direct from the mouth of the Prophet any part of the Quran now bring it here to us". They had written what they had heard on sheets, tablets and palm-branches. Umar would not accept anything from anyone until two witnesses bore testimony.

He was assassinated while still engaged on his collection. His successor, Uthman addressed the people, "Let whoever has anything of the Book of God bring it here to us". Uthman would accept nothing from anyone until two witnesses bore testimony. .... [9]

A tradition also indicates that Hudhayfa was concerned before the expedition

Hudhayfa said, "The Kufans say, 'the text of Abdullah' [Ibn Mas'ud]; the Basrans say, 'the text of Abu Musa'. By God! if I reach the Commander of the faithful, I will recommend that he drown these

readings". Abdullah [Ibn Mas'ud] said, "Do and God will drown you, but not in water!" [10]

Generally True

In support of a general truth underlying the Uthman traditions, Gregor Schoeler, the modern Western scholar, says *"after a certain time, circumstances must have rendered it necessary to produce a single and generally binding version of the holy book"* and he makes two arguments that particularly support the proposition that Uthman did this. [11]

Firstly, while there is much uncertainty and disagreement over who was the first to commission a collection of the Quran, whether it was Abu Bakr, Umar or Uthman, it is widely agreed that Uthman was the first to order and distribute an official version.

Secondly, there are both traditions highly critical of what Uthman did and traditions full of praise for his achievement.

Established Quran readers and their supporters were reluctant to recognise a single version of the Quran from Uthman. His version was simply one among many. This opposition to Uthman is seen in the way he was reproached by later rebels who said: *"The Quran was (many) books You have given them up except for one"* [12]

Another tradition has the rebels saying:

"You have burned the book of God" He replied: "People read (the Quran) in different ways one would say: 'My Quran is better than yours' The other would say: 'no, mine is better '" [ ] They said: "But why did you burn the (other) collections?" [ ] He replied: "I wanted nothing else to exist except what had been written in front of the Messenger of God, and was contained in the pages of Hafsa". [13]

On the other hand, various traditions are favourable and outstanding praise comes from Ali, the Prophet's cousin and son-in-law, who is reported to have said: *"If Uthman had not done this, I would have done it".* [14]

The statement attributed to Ali may be a fabrication designed to boost support for Uthman who was not a very popular caliph, but if this was the case, that people took the trouble to invent such stories, the accusations they were meant to dispel, must have existed!

There was a genuine controversy over something that really happened. It is most unlikely that the originators of the report of Uthman's creation and distribution of a standard Quran would also create reports defending his actions against accusations which had not yet been made.

Another supporting factor identified by Schoeler concerns the many reports of the continued existence of variants even of Uthman's standard version distributed to the major Islamic centres. Such variants arise naturally as a result of the hand-written production of copies and it seems most unlikely that anyone would fabricate a report about variants to support another fabrication, that Uthman's official version was a fabrication!

Collective memory is another argument for an historical core to the various Uthman collection and codification traditions. [15] Uthman's codex is remembered not only in the cities it was sent to but across all the diverse and sometimes clashing religious communities of early Islam such as the proto-Shi'a, and Companions who continued to transmit their variants did not deny the origin of the standard version. People would know under which caliph they received the Quran and it would be very difficult for any authority to later eradicate this knowledge and name another caliph.

One Among Many

It is important to understand the text chosen by Uthman as the official version of the Quran was only one of several texts existing at the time, and though there are plenty of reports that Zayd was a leading and well-qualified figure for work on collecting and compiling the Quran, the text he produced, whether under Abu Bakr or Uthman, cannot be regarded as more correct than that produced by others such as the Companions Ibn Mas'ud, Ubayy b.

Ka'b or Abu Musa. And, none of the collections can be said to be the authorised text of Muhammad himself. [16]

It is also very likely that there were important divergences between all the collections that had become established in the great centres of Medina, Mecca, Basra, Kufa and Damascus and this is why Uthman took the drastic action of ordering the destruction of all other copies with no exemptions.

Arthur Jeffery made the point *"Now when we come to the accounts of Uthman's recension, it quickly becomes clear that his work was no mere matter of removing dialectal peculiarities in reading, but was a necessary stroke of policy to establish a standard text for the whole empire".* [Arthur Jeffery, *Materials For The History Of The Text Of The Quran*, p8]

Reactions of Companions

Uthman's order to destroy all other copies of the Quran so only his version would be available was fiercely opposed in some quarters.

Ibn Mas'ud whose codex had become the authoritative copy of the Quran in Kufa was angry that Uthman ordered the destruction of his codex, saying his version was just as valid as Uthman's or any other collection. He refused to hand it over for destruction. He even told his students to conceal their copies so they would not be destroyed.

Al-Zuhri also narrated that Abdullah Ibn Mas'ud became upset because he was not chosen to copy the Quran. He said, "Oh you Muslims, how can I not be chosen ..." Ibn Mas'ud also said, "Oh people of Iraq! Hide your Qurans in your homes (from Uthman)". [17]

Other traditions make clear Ibn Mas'ud believed his knowledge of the Quran was greatly superior to that of Zayd. He, Ibn Mas'ud, had become a Muslim in Mecca even before Zayd was born and had been a close companion of Muhammad for many years.

The people have been guilty of deceit in the reading of the Quran. I like it better to read according to the recitation of him (Prophet) whom I love more than that of Zayd b. Thabit. By Him besides Whom there is no god! I learnt more than seventy suras from the lips of the Apostle of Allah, may Allah bless him, while Zayd b. Thabit was a youth, having two locks and playing with the youth. [18]

Further sayings of Ibn Mas'ud regarding how he perceived his Quranic knowledge and expertise are given above in Chapter 3, Companion Codices.

Abu Musa, the compiler of another famous Companion's codex, seems to have accepted the validity of Uthman's version but believed his codex was still just as valuable. What he says also suggests the differences were more than those generated by different dialects or pronunciation.

I went to Abu Musa's house and saw there Abdullah and Hudhayfa. I sat with them. They had a mushaf that Uthman had sent ordering them to make their Quran conform with it. Abu Musa declared that anything in his mushaf and lacking in Uthman's was not to be omitted. Anything in Uthman's and lacking in his own was to be added. .... [19]

~~~~

Chapter 5 – Variants

We see above that Uthman's purpose was to have only one version of the Quran. There would be no variants! It is important at this point to explain the nature of variants and how they arise. When studying the history of the Quran it is important to understand exactly what is meant by the term.

How Variants Arise

(1) Human Factors

If you ask several people what they have just heard someone say, it is not a surprise if their replies are not exactly the same.

Such human factors can lead to different ways of saying the same thing, synonyms, different word sequences, different words, different phrases, and the addition and omission of words and sentences, when a speaker's words are repeated by others.

Even an experienced scribe may not produce a one hundred per cent accurate copy of the words during a dictation or make an exact copy of a text. The organisation and sequence of content is also subject to human factors.

(2) Orality

Modern research has shown there is a fundamental difference between oral and written literature. Yasin Dutton explains this is especially relevant for the Quran revealed in a society where oral communication was the norm and writing played little part. [1] Oral literature is multiform. For example, a poem, which has never been written down, may be recited on different occasions with considerable but minor changes that don't affect the basic story or message. To both the reciter and audience this is perfectly normal. Variation was accepted and might not even have been noticed.

The Quran is much more than poetry, of course, but it as an oral phenomenon. The word, "Quran", means recitation and it is most likely to have been received and used as other oral works were in early Arabian oral culture. It is also likely that Muhammad himself introduced different forms by reciting passages at different times in slightly different ways as indicated by tradition and in the Quran where stories are repeated with slightly different wording. [2]

(3) The Writing System – A Defective Script

In the early stages of the development of the Arabic script, during the first Islamic century and even later, Arabic was written in what experts call a *scriptio defectiva*. This technical term means the script was not able to represent in writing all the sounds of spoken Arabic.

Early written Arabic lacked markings or signs for vowels and showed only consonants. To complicate matters, there were only 17 signs with which to represent 28 consonants so some signs could stand for more than one consonant, and diacritics in the form of dots above or below ambiguous signs were introduced to indicate exactly what consonant a sign represented.

Though we lack manuscripts from Uthman's time and earlier, research shows diacritics were almost certainly used in such early Quran manuscripts but sparsely and inconsistently. They are found used in this way in inscriptions and papyri of that early time. The earliest surviving examples are two administrative papyri dated to 643 CE (22 AH) and an inscription dated to 645 CE (24 AH). François Déroche noted that a folio of a Quranic manuscript dated to the first century AH contained eight dotted signs whereas the equivalent modern text has 240. [3]

Over time, signs for long vowels and marks to show the position of short vowels were introduced and there was a more consistent and comprehensive use of diacritics to distinguish consonants but it took several centuries for a complete and standard script to be established.

With the *scriptio defectiva* system in use in Uthman's time, verbs could be taken as active or passive, nouns could have different case endings and some could be read as either a noun or a verb. The reader had to decide the correct word and how it should be said from the context or memory of the spoken text. For example, the *rasm*, the consonantal form, showing "ql" could be read "qala", meaning "he said", or "qul", meaning "say", and even "qalla", "to be or become little, small, few".

The role of the writing system might be thought of as a sophisticated set of mnemonics rather than as a way of accurately recording speech.

All these features introduced uncertainty in the reading of early Qurans though it was not necessarily a big problem as the correct reading of the great majority of words could be determined by the context and syntax. And, in the early years of Islam, memory and oral transmission dominated Quranic teaching and public recitations were not given from a written manuscript. [4]

Nevertheless, the text was read and recited in many different ways and some of the variations affected the meaning of particular phrases or sentences though not the underlying ideas of the Quran.

Very Early Islam – Different Recitations

Reports of different recitations of the Quran go back to the time of the Prophet and it is clear Muslims experienced and found ways to cope with variant readings of the Quran from the beginning. Traditions explain that the differences were permitted by the Prophet. The Quran was revealed to him in multiple ways though unfortunately, the traditions do not explain the nature of the differences. [5]

Here are some examples of the hadiths that cover this.

Narrated Umar b. Al-Khattab: I heard Hisham b. Hakim b. Hizam reciting Sura al-Furqan in a way different to that of mine. Allah's Messenger had taught it to me (in a different way). So, I was about to quarrel with him (during the prayer) but I waited till he finished, then I tied his garment round his neck and seized him by it and brought him to Allah's Messenger and said, "I have heard him reciting Sura al-Furqan in a way different to the way you taught it to me". The Prophet ordered me to release him and asked Hisham to recite it. When he recited it,

Allah's Apostle said, "It was revealed in this way". He then asked me to recite it. When I recited it, he said, "It was revealed in this way. The Quran has been revealed in seven different ways, so recite it in the way that is easier for you". [al-Bukhari 2419, Book 44, Hadith 9 / Vol. 3, Book 41, Hadith 601]

Ibn Abbas reported Allah's Messenger as saying: Gabriel taught me to recite in one style. I replied to him and kept asking him to give more (styles), till he reached seven modes (of recitation). Ibn Shibab said: It has reached me that these seven styles are essentially one, not differing about what is permitted and what is forbidden. [Muslim 819a, Book 6, Hadith 330 / Book 4, Hadith 1785]

Ubayy b. Ka'b reported that the Messenger of Allah was near the tank of Banu Ghifar that Gabriel came to him and said: Allah has commanded you to recite to your people the Quran in one dialect. Upon this he said: I ask from Allah pardon and forgiveness. My people are not capable of doing it. He then came for the second time and said: Allah has commanded you that you should recite the Quran to your people in two dialects. Upon this he (the Holy Prophet) again said: I seek pardon and forgiveness from Allah, my people would not be able to do so. He (Gabriel) came for the third time and said: Allah has commanded you to recite the Quran to your people in three dialects. Upon this he said: I ask pardon and forgiveness from Allah. My people would not be able to do it. He then came to him for the fourth time and said: Allah has commanded you to recite the Quran to your people in seven dialects, and in whichever dialect they would recite, they would be right. [Muslim 821a, Book 6, Hadith 334 / Book 4, Hadith 1789]

These hadiths showing the Prophet approved of the Quran being recited in different ways or dialects, highlights one of the puzzles about early Islam. If different dialects were acceptable why did Uthman specify the standard Quran that he ordered should be in the Quraysh dialect and that all Qurans that did not conform should be destroyed. He was, apparently, going against the word of Muhammad himself.

The Muslim term for these seven ways of reciting the Quran is *sabati ahruf*. There are various interpretations of the word "*ahruf*".

The term is a plural of *"harf"* usually taken to mean "letter" or groups of letters. The interpretation that *ahruf* refers to tribal dialects is undermined by an important example of two Companions disagreeing over a Quran recitation who were from the same tribe and thus spoke in the same dialect. Though very little is known about these seven ways and all we have are the reported variant recitations of various Companions, the fact of the existence of different ways gives strong support to the oral and multiform view of the Quran mentioned above. Today's canonical variant readings are discussed in Chapter 13.

After Uthman

The text disseminated by Uthman was in the Arabic *scriptio defectiva,* the writing system of his period. It did not solve the problem of variants introduced by such a defective writing system.

That there were many other kinds of variants in the early decades of Islam is made clear by the various works and commentaries on the Quran that soon followed. [These works are discussed in Chapter 8, Early Islamic Literature.] They cover the whole range of possible variants including the use of synonyms, changes of word order, the insertion or absence of words and phrases, and the addition or omission of material. This is what Hudhayfa's soldiers must have been arguing over! [6] Various Muslim traditions describe how whole sections of the Quran may have been lost or removed. [Chapter 9 covers variants said to be found in Companion codices and Chapter 10 the relevant Muslim traditions.]

The fact that in standardising the Quran into a single text Uthman demanded that all other copies of the Quran should be destroyed suggests the problem was serious. It took determination and conviction to burn Companion codices, the revealed word of God, carefully recorded by the Prophet's closest Companions, some copies of which had become the authoritative Quran in one of the metropolitan centres of the expanding Islamic empire.

Uthman's standardisation reduced text variations but multiple readings still occurred, not just because of the *scriptio defectiva* but because the official copies sent to the metropolitan centres were not all identical; they contained copying mistakes brought about by the carelessness of scribes and a lack of careful supervision. Further copying produced more variants. Most of the differences may have been minor but they made changes in the *rasm*.

A tradition reports that when the copies to be distributed were shown to Uthman for his approval he noted incorrect words or passages but said *"Do not change them, the Arabs will change them"*, and in other versions of the tradition, *"They will change them with their tongues"*, or *"The Arabs will pronounce them correctly"*. [7]

It was also inevitable the writing system should improve. The Islamic community was greatly expanding bringing in new peoples and transmission and recitation of the Quran could not continue to rely on memorisation, and this helped bring about the introduction and greater use of writing signs to show vowels and distinguish consonants—vowel marks and diacritical points above and below the relevant consonants—a *scriptio plena* that accurately showed exactly what should be read. [8]

This meant throughout the Umayyad period (661–750 CE) and into Abbasid times (750+ CE) work continued on the text of the Quran opening up the possibility of variations and changes. To complicate matters there existed still elements of the Companion codices especially of Ibn Mas'ud and Ubayy and there is considerable debate over when and by whom the text of the Quran was finally codified.

Chapter 11 covers what might have happened to the Quran up to and in the time of the famous Umayyad caliph, Abd al-Malik.

~~~~

Chapter 6 – Reliability of Traditions

The various Abu Bakr and Uthman traditions given above explaining how the Quran was collected are reports passed orally from one generation to the next until they were eventually written down. Traditions are also known as hadiths.

A hadith has two parts: the words of the report itself, the *matn*; and the *isnad*, the chain of persons—transmitters—who passed it orally from the original witness of the words or actions to the scholar who finally wrote it down in a hadith collection. [1]

Hadiths cover all aspects of life in the early years of Islam. The most famous hadith collector is al-Bukhari (194–256 AH) who made his collection some 200 years after the time of the words or actions reported and thus the reports had passed word-of-mouth through six generations or so before being written down. Al-Bukhari's most famous work has over 7000 hadiths.

There are dozens of hadith collections. Al-Bukhari, and Muslim, also very famous like al-Bukhari, plus four others make up the canonical six all produced between 200–300 AH. [See ANNEX 1]

Hadiths with a *matn* giving different versions of the same event are frequently repeated within the same collection and in different collections. The report is much the same but the *isnad* is different, and each version counts as a separate hadith. Al-Bukhari's collection of 7000 hadiths, in fact, covers only 2500 or so distinct accounts or events.

There is a wide range of views on the reliability of hadiths. Early modern Western scholars believed hadiths were largely fabricated. They were the result of those living 150 or more years after the Prophet, when the written hadith collections were created, projecting their ideas and beliefs back onto the Prophet and his time.

Hadiths are found with anachronisms. There are hadiths that concern rivalry for the caliphate and obviously have a political motive. One such hadith thought to be circulated by the supporters of Ali has the Prophet saying *"If you see Mu'awiya ascend my pulpit, then kill him"*. [2] Mu'awiya was the caliph who established the Umayyad dynasty and his followers produced hadiths supporting him and against Ali. There are contradictory hadiths. For example, there are traditions saying the Prophet supported the written recording of his sayings and deeds, and others saying he forbade all such writing except when it concerned his revelations.

It is also striking that some of the reports traced back to the Prophet in later hadith collections can be found in earlier collections traced back only to a Successor or Companion; it was their belief or deed. This backward growth of *isnads* may have taken place on a large scale. [3]

Some Western scholars believed all hadiths were unreliable while others thought they still contained a useful core of historical information.

Whatever the view of hadiths a remarkable phenomenon occurs when the *isnads* of the *matns* of different versions of the same event are illustrated together in a bundle; a common link appears (along with several partial common links). See Diagram 1

Some Western scholars claim the common link is the result of forgery. In reality, there was no common link. A hadith collector is the first to fabricate and circulate a particular hadith going back to a supposed source. Some of his peers copy it but give a different name for the person who they heard it from, so it appears to come to them from a different route. Later other fabricators invent completely new transmission lines going back to the same source, now appearing as a common link. Hadith forgeries are known and something like this could happen but it involves a lot of people systematically going to a lot of trouble.

It seems much more likely that the common link is a real person. He might be a fabricator making up the story himself or, on the other hand, simply be the first to collect the story, a genuine story, and teach it to others.

Diagram 1 – The Common Link

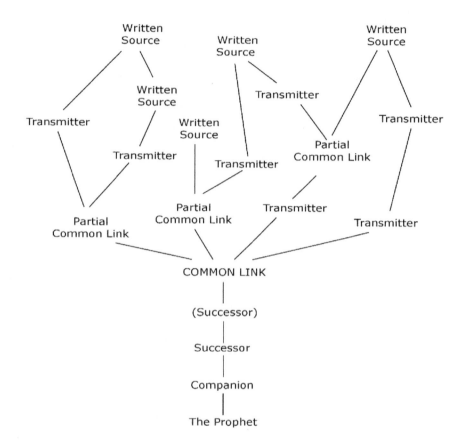

A New Research Method

Fairly recently, by the standards of Islamic historical research, a method has been developed which throws some light on the validly of a hadith; were those words really spoken, did that event really happen, at least as far as the common link is concerned.

Western scholars developed a new method to investigate the origins and authenticity of hadiths, starting as far back as the 1950s but coming into most prominence in the 1990s and recent decades. The principles of the method, *isnad-cum-matn-analysis* (ICMA) were first formally outlined in works published in 1996 by Gregor

Schoeler and Harald Motzki. They both highlighted the need to examine *matns* together with their *isnads* and how they related to one another.

The variations in the different versions of a hadith *matn* coming via different *isnad* chains from a common link are most likely the result of how each *matn* was handled by the transmitters in the *isnad* chain going back to the common link.

Variations can take many forms; items added, items omitted, and textual features, for example. If there is a common core—common archetype—for all the versions of that hadith that can be traced back to and identified with a common link, then that common link is very likely to be the genuine source of that common archetype.

He did transmit that hadith. If there is still only a single strand below the confirmed common link back to the time of the Prophet methods other than ICMA are needed to evaluate that single strand and determine the origin of the hadith.

What Motzki Did and His Results

In a paper, *The Collection of the Quran - A Reconsideration of Western Views in Light of Recent Methodological Developments* [4] published in 2001, Motzki examines both the Abu Bakr and Uthman traditions concerning how they each were involved in organising a complete copy of the Quran and in Uthman's case standardising it.

Motzki identifies 11 hadith sources that give 18 versions of the Abu Bakr collection hadith. The *isnads* of all the *matns* of these hadith versions go back to a common link, one Ibn Shibab al-Zuhri (d. 124 AH)(742 CE). Patterns emerge. The groupings of the variations in all these *matns* and how they match up to *isnads* suggest a common archetype, a common ancestor so to speak, confirming al-Zuhri as a genuine common link who transmitted the hadith.

For Uthman, Motzki identifies eight hadith sources that give 16 versions of the Uthman hadith. All the *isnads* go back to a common link, the same Ibn Shibab al-Zuhri, and again the variations in the *matns* and how they relate to the *isnads* show there must have been a single source for all those *matns*. Ibn Shibab al-Zuhri is the source for all of them.

Thus, we can be reasonably certain reports on a collection of the Quran on Abu Bakr's behalf and an official edition made by order of Uthman were already in circulation in the first quarter of the second century AH, during al-Zuhri's lifetime.

Table 1 lists the hadith sources used by Motzki and indicates when the hadiths were first recorded in written form by a collector.

Table 1 – Motzki's Sources

Sources for Abu Bakr Tradition		Sources for Uthman Tradition	
Hadith Collection	Lifetime AH of Collector	Hadith Collection	Lifetime AH of Collector
al-Tayalisi	133–204	al-Tabari	224–310
Abd al-Razzaq	126–211	al-Nas'ai	224–303
al-Bukhari	194–256	Ibn Shabba	d. 264
Abu Ubayd	155–224	Abu Ya'la	d. 307
Ibn Hanbal	164–241	Ibn Abi Dawud	d. 316
Musa b. Uqba	55–141	al-Tirmidhi	209–279
al-Tabari	224–310	Abu Ubayd	155–224
al-Nas'ai	224–303	al-Bukhari	194–256
Abu Ya'la	d. 307		
Ibn Abi Dawud	d. 316		
al-Tirmidhi	209–279		

Al-Zuhri was a famous scholar and teacher and a prolific collector of stories about the life of the Prophet and of other traditions. He came from Medina and moved to Damascus to work on Islamic legal matters and while there joined the administration of the caliph, Abd al-Malik. He rose to high positions under the following caliphs, Umar II and Hisham (r. 105–125 AH) and composed a book or notebook for the library of the Umayyad court and became tutor to the princes under Hisham.

In his paper, Motzki reproduces three detailed *isnad* bundle diagrams, two covering Abu Bakr and one Uthman, for all the hadiths in the sources he investigated

Diagram 1 is a simplified form of Motzki's bundle diagrams. It highlights al-Zuhri and the single strands that go back to the person who he claims is the contemporary eyewitness and author of the account of what the caliphs did.

Unfortunately, there is no accepted method of establishing the validity of these single strands. If the lives of those mentioned in the strand did not overlap it would show a strand must be false but otherwise deciding if a strand is most likely to be valid, depends on circumstances and what one judges to be corroborating evidence. Motzki notes there are other Quran collection reports transmitted by al-Zuhri that come from other members of the generation of Abu Bakr and Uthman's time. He takes the view:

.... *the common links which belong to the generation of al-Zuhri and the following generation should not necessarily be considered as originators of the traditions but as the first systematic collectors of traditions who transmitted them to regular classes of students out of which an institutionalised system of learning developed.*

Significance of the Results

That accounts of Abu Bakr's and Uthman's involvement in the collection of the Quran can be convincingly dated to the first quarter of the second century AH undermines the radical theory that the Quran was not put together until much later. This theory was suggested by Wansbrough's analysis in his books *Quranic Studies* and *The Sectarian Milieu* published in 1977 and 1978. [5]

On the other hand, Motzki's findings still leave open the question of how the Quran was created and put together in the early decades. One can still debate the accuracy of the hadith transmitted by al-Zuhri. There are still different accounts. And, they do not rule out the view that the Quran was not finally and successfully standardised until the time of the caliph, Abd al-Malik (r. 685–705 CE) [6]

Other Analysis of Traditions Transmitted by al-Zuhri

That al-Zuhri is a genuine transmitter of traditions is also revealed by ICMA analysis of 270 variants of three traditions where he is again the common link, carried out by Nicolet Boekhoff-van der Voort in her PhD thesis (2012) *Between History and Legend: The Biography of the Prophet Muhammad by Ibn Shihab al-Zuhri.*

The three traditions concern the biography of the Prophet; his miraculous night journey to Jerusalem, and two military raids, one by Muslims and the other against them. Not all the variants are accounted for by transmission differences or transitions in al-Zuhri's teaching style and it seems al-Zuhri may have edited his material with the insertion of embellishments, names of persons, as well as explanatory words and elements. ICMA applied to *sira* material shows the *"biography of the Prophet Muhammad more specifically bears the imprint of the person who transmitted the story"*.

~~~~

Chapter 7 – Early Writing and Compilation

Evidence for Writing and the Prophet's Role

Other traditions make clear Quranic revelations were put into writing. Al-Suyuti (d. 911 AH)(1505 CE) says even though the Quran was not put together in one place all the separate revelations were written down and carefully stored. One might also surmise where revelations concerned legal matters it was important to have them written down. [1]

Revelations varied greatly in length from just a verse or two to longer pieces and Muslim and Western scholars believe most of the Quran's suras, its chapters, are compositions of separate revelations that are not necessarily linked to one another or in sequence.

There is no clear understanding of how the suras were put together though another tradition found in al-Suyuti says the Prophet had a hand and writing was involved. In the later stages of revelation *"When [Muhammad] received a revelation, he would summon one of those who acted as his scribes and say, 'Put this passage in the sura in which so-and-so is mentioned', or 'Put it in such-and-such a place'"*. [2]

Another tradition that concerns Umar, the man who became the second caliph, speaks of written Quranic material. He heard his sister reading a portion of Sura 20 from a written sheet. This angered him and he struck her but then relented and said, *"Give me this sheet which I heard you reading just now so that I may see just what it is which Muhammad has brought"*. After reading it he went to Muhammad and became a Muslim. There are different versions of this story and another version has Umar discovering someone reading the text to his sister and he does not hit her. [3]

If the story is based on a real event it shows at least some parts of the Quran were written down in the early period of Islam in Mecca. There are contradictory accounts of Umar's conversion and that Sura 20 was in circulation as early as that time may be an anachronism but even if the story is a dramatic fabrication, the fabricator thought it credible to talk about early written Quranic material.

A number of traditions attest the Prophet employed secretaries and scribes when he was in Medina and some of the scribes were used to write down Quranic revelations. There is a remarkable story about one of them, Abdullah b. Sa'd b. Abi Sarh.

In the course of dictating a Quranic passage describing the creation of man to Abdullah, Muhammad paused after the words "another creature" so overcome was he with wonder at the description. Abdullah interjected and pronounced aloud *"Blessed be Allah, best of creators"*. Muhammad told him those indeed were the words of the revelation and Abdullah should complete the verse with those words. This apparently casual or chance formation of Quranic material so disturbed Abdullah that he became an apostate and returned to Mecca.

He was later taken prisoner after the capture of Mecca but spared on the intercession of Uthman. This story about Abdullah who was an Umayyad could be seen as anti-Umayyad propaganda and a fabrication but according to some Western scholars, it was very unlikely such propaganda would have been produced that could also be seen as critical of the Prophet. [4]

Schoeler's Explanation of Early Practice

Gregor Schoeler, a leading Western scholar, throws an interesting light on the possible balance between the writing of Quranic material and its dependence on oral transmission. According to tradition, the Prophet repeated the revelations he received to suitable individuals he trusted to memorise them and repeat them when he was not present. [5] These persons became known as *qurra* (reciters).

This method of dissemination already existed in Arabia for Arabic poetry. Arab poets did not write down their works, they depended on *rawi* (transmitters) and there is a strong parallel between *qurra* and *rawi*. Schoeler says:

It may be that in the earliest period the Prophet did not regard it as necessary that the revelations be written down. When, however, they became more frequent and longer (probably several years before the Hijra), it was only natural that they would be committed to writing Muhammad began to dictate the revelations to literate persons (kuttab al-wahy), either to those he designated as scribes ad hoc (such as Uthman, Mu'awiya, Ubayy b. Ka'b, Zayd b. Thabit, Abdullah b. Sa'd b. Abi Sarh), or to the secretaries responsible for his correspondence. [6]

Some of the scribes were also *qurra* and one of them Ubayy b. Ka'b became well-known for having a complete copy of the Quran. [7] [See Chapter 3]

It thus seems possible that a large part, if not most, of the Quran, had been written down on proper sheets by the time of the Prophet's death, with a smaller part, still not in proper written form but recorded on various other materials. This is consistent with the picture given by traditional accounts of the state of Quranic material when the Prophet died.

Schoeler goes on to say putting the Quran into written form must have been considered much more important and necessary than it would have been for doing the same for poetry and there is Western scholarly opinion that given the nature of the revelations, the Prophet soon believed it was of the greatest importance to have a book as other "people of the book" had theirs, and this was the ultimate purpose of the growing Quran. [8] [See also Bell's argument mentioned below.]

However, it is still very unclear what role the Prophet himself played in producing a complete and final version of the Quran. As noted above authors and poets at the time of early Islam and for centuries later did not redact or publish their own work and Quranic revelations were continuing and even subject to change.

The Prophet's Role in Compilation

Two hadiths, in particular, suggest the Prophet played a key role in the compilation of the Quran.

One states: *The Prophet was the most generous of all the people, and he used to become more generous in Ramadan when Gabriel met him. Gabriel used to meet him every night during Ramadan to revise the Quran with him. ....* [al-Bukhari 3554, Book 61, Hadith 63 / Book 56, Hadith 754]

The other says: *.... I asked her what the Prophet had told her. She said, "I would never disclose the secret of Allah's Messenger". When the Prophet died, I asked her about it. She replied. "The Prophet said: 'Every year Gabriel used to revise the Quran with me once only, but this year he has done so twice. I think this portends my death, and you will be the first of my family to follow me'". ....* [al-Bukhari 3623, 3624, Book 61, Hadith 129 / Book 56, Hadith 819]

Both hadiths imply there was divinely inspired editorial input and the second also implies there was the deliberate creation of a complete and final text put together in a particular way even if it was not necessarily given written form. [9] The Quran had some shape and organisation at the time of the Prophet's death. If this was the case why did it have to be collected from a wide variety of materials and the memories of individuals?

Richard Bell

Richard Bell is famous for his translation of the Quran published in 1937 and the chronological order he gave the suras. Another well-known work of his *An introduction to the Quran* was updated and rewritten by W. Montgomery Watt and published in 1970. [10] Bell argues the Prophet played a much greater part in writing and compiling the Quran than traditions allow.

Muhammad Could Read and Write

Early Muslims were challenged by those who did not follow Islam for having no miracles to prove the truth of their religion, and they responded by saying the Quran itself was a miracle. Consequently, it became necessary to portray Muhammad, who communicated the Quran, as a man who could neither read nor write. That he could read and write cannot be demonstrated but there is substantial circumstantial evidence that he could.

There is a Quranic reference to Muhammad using a word that can be interpreted to mean "unlettered" and this is used to prove his illiteracy but the word can also be interpreted to mean he had not read certain texts, in this case, Jewish and Christian scriptures. The tradition describing his first revelation gives another ambiguous case. Some versions have the Prophet saying, *"I cannot recite"* as if he was illiterate, others have him saying *"What shall I recite"*.

Another tradition has him making alterations in his own hand to the Treaty of al-Hudaybiya in 628 CE. The Meccans wanted to remove the reference to "Messenger of God" and when Ali, acting as secretary, refused to do this Muhammad himself replaced it in his own hand with his family name.

The fact that Muhammad was a merchant for many years is very strong circumstantial evidence. It is hard to imagine a merchant who needs to keep accounts and records and who travels widely, could not read or write to some degree.

The Written Materials Were Given Form

Bell carried out a detailed examination of each sura noting such aspects as changes in grammatical construction, rhyming schemes and content and concluded that nearly all suras were constructed from numerous and originally separate passages. There were very few lengthy compositions. Bell said:

.... Once we have caught the lilt of Quran style it becomes fairly easy to separate the suras into separate pieces of which they have been built up. [Watt and Bell 1970: 73]

Bell's analysis enabled him to argue the work of composition of suras could be divided into three main periods:

1. An early period producing mainly signs and exhortations to worship God. Only fragments of this period survived.

2. A Quran period during which the main purpose was to create a "recitation" (quran) concentrating on the messages of previous revelations. This covered the late part of Muhammad's time in Mecca and the first year or so of his time in Medina.

3. A book period in which Muhammad is producing a *kitab* (a book) that would be independent of revelation. [11]

Bell stresses that originally the word "quran" denoted the recitation of one or more passages. It was most probably derived from a Syriac word meaning a scriptural reading or lesson in church. The word is used mainly in the early suras. In later suras the word *kitab* takes over. Though it had more than one meaning, it means "book" and indicates the idea of producing a book as possessed by other religions became important.

The idea of producing a book on papyrus is given some support in the Quran. Q 6:7 suggests that Muhammad had this in mind and *suhaf* (single writing sheets) are linked with revelations in Q 20:133; 53:37; 80:13; 87:18, and 98:2. And, when the accusation is made in Q 25:6-7 that the Quran is written down this is not denied.

The noted Western scholar Arthur Jeffery said *".... there is internal evidence in the Quran itself that the Prophet kept in his own care a considerable mass of revelation material belonging to various periods of his activity, some of it in revised and some of it in unrevised form, and that this material was to form the basis of the Kitab he wished to give his community before he died. Death, however, overtook him before anything was done about the matter".* [12]

A remarkable indication of early composition by Muhammad is given by the various Companion codices. [See Chapter 3] If there hadn't been some early sura composition then the early Companion codices would have reflected this with Companions memorising different passages and putting them together differently. Though there are various differences between the early Companion codices, they display remarkable similarity of the order of what makes up different suras.

Bell argued that when Zayd b. Thabit started his collection on behalf of the caliph much of the Quran was in written form and that some could have been written by Muhammad himself. Bell is not saying collectors did nothing; it is a matter of degree.

Muhammad's suras were not identical with present suras and there would have been no fixed order. The collectors added to these embryonic suras at appropriate points any verses or short passages not included that they found on miscellaneous written materials or recorded in the "hearts of men". Montgomery Watt states *"One would think that at most the material to be added might be as much again, and at the least perhaps one-fifth of the bulk of the suras".*

~~~~

PART 2

THE TEXT

Chapter 8 – Early Muslim Literature

Introduction
The question of variants plays a big part in the collection process, and variants covered more than the differences caused by the use of an early and defective script.

This chapter introduces a body of early Islamic literature that in various ways mentioned, discussed or analysed differences in early versions of the text of the Quran. The following two chapters give examples and indicate some of the possibilities.

Early Works
Al-Nadim (d. 384 AH), a famous Muslim librarian, made a catalogue, *The Fihrist,* of all the books in Arabic in the year 375 AH. They include the works that indirectly provide much of what we know about Companion codices. He listed 11 works that examined or mentioned the differences between versions of the Quran under the following two headings. [1]

Discrepancies of the Quranic Manuscripts (*Ikhtilaf al-Masahif*)
al-Kisai (d. 189 AH). *Discrepancies between the Manuscripts of the People of Madina, Kufa, and Basra*

Abu Zakariya al-Farra (d. 207 AH). *Discrepancies of the People of Kufa, Basra, and Syria concerning the Manuscripts*

al-Madaini (d. c. 231 AH). *Book of al-Madaini about the discrepancies between the manuscripts and the compiling of the Quran*

Ibn Amir al-Yahsubi (d. 118 AH). *Discrepancies between the Manuscripts of Syria, the Hijaz, and Iraq*

Plus four other such works, and three simply called Book of Quran codices.

Book of Quran Codices (*Kitab al-Masahif*)
Ibn Abi Dawud (d. 316 AH) *Kitab al-Masahif*

Ibn al-Anbari (d. 328 AH), and

Ibn Ashta al-Isfahani (d. 360 AH).

The only work of all the above to survive into modern times is that of Ibn Abi Dawud discovered by the famous Western scholar Arthur Jeffery and published in 1937 which unfortunately was probably the least informative in its range of topics. The number of variants it gives is small and most of them are found in other works but it mentions and draws attention to a good number of Companion codices. Ibn Abi Dawud was the son of Abu Dawud the compiler of one of the famous six canonical hadith collections. (See below)

Some early and orthodox Muslim scholars have argued that where authors such as Ibn Abi Dawud referred to variants in "*mushafs*" they were really referring to variants in readings not written material. The phrase "to collect the Quran" simply meant "to remember the whole of the Quran". Jeffery makes several strong points that the references were to written codices; for example, why would Uthman have ordered the burning of copies and why is there a report that Ali brought along what he had collected on the back of his camel.

We know something about what the lost works said and the information they provided because they were used by later Muslim scholars in their works that have survived.

The last two mentioned above seemed to have been the most comprehensive and highly regarded by later Muslim scholars, especially Ibn al-Anbari's work. Each work studied the collection, orthography, and understanding of Uthman's text and discussed what was known about the Companion codices it replaced.

Other Works Concerning the Quran – Interpretation and Commentary

These works concern the interpretation (*tafsir*) and meaning of the Quran including the meaning of unusual words and the correct understanding of the grammar. The larger ones especially refer to the Companion codices and non-canonical readings providing useful information about them.

The earliest and extant commentary is the great work of the historian Muhammad b. Jarir al-Tabari which when printed in Cairo in 1903 occupied thirty volumes. For most verses al-Tabari gives his own interpretation and quotes earlier authorities giving the chain of transmitters through whom it has reached him.

al-Tabari (224–310 AH). *Tafsir al-Quran (Commentary on the Quran)*

al-Zamakhshari (d. 538 AH). *Al-Kashshaf (The Revealer)*

al-Baydawi (d. 685 AH). *Anwar al-Tansil wa Asrar al-Tawil (The Lights of Revelation and the Secrets of Interpretation)*

Fakhr al-Din al-Razi (544–606 AH). *Tafsir al-Kabir (The Large Commentary)*

Ibn al-Jawzi (d. 597 AH).

Abu Hayyan al-Gharnati (654–745 AH). *Tafsir al-Bahr al-Muhit (The Explanation Ocean; Commentary on the linguistic meanings of the Quran).*

al-Qurtubi (d. 671 AH). *al-Jami' li-Ahkam al-Quran*

Other Works - Readings and Language
Works covering canonical and non-canonical Quran readings and Arabic language and grammar also provide information.

al-Farra (d. 207 AH). *Kitab Maani al-Quran*

Ibn Khalawayh (d. 370 AH). *Mukhtasar*

Ibn Jinni (d. 392 AH). *Muhtasab*

Later Scholars
A notable example of the use of earlier sources in the work of a later scholar is the famous works of al-Suyuti (849–911 AH). (1) al-Itqan fi Ulum al-Quran (Perfect Guide to the Sciences of the Quran), (2) al-Durr al-Manthur fi al-Tafsir al-Mathur, (3) al-Muzhir.

Jeffery's Sources

In his famous work *Materials for the History of the Text of the Quran* that lists all the known variants in 15 primary Companion codices, Arthur Jeffery identifies the 31 sources he found and used that gave this information. [See ANNEX 2]

Hadiths

Another important source for information on Companion codices and questions about the contents of the Quran are the canonical six hadith collections. [2] [See Chapter 6 and ANNEX 1 for an explanation of hadiths.]

Sahih al-Bukhari (194–256 AH)
Sahih Muslim (204–261 AH)
Sunan Abu Dawud (202–275 AH)
Jami' al-Tirmidhi (209–279 AH)
Sunan al-Nas'ai (224–303 AH)
Sunan Ibn Majah (209–273 AH)

The first two listed, al-Bukhari and Muslim, were the first hadith collections in which all the hadiths included met certain authenticity requirements. These two collections also became the most famous and are known as the *Sahihan*, "the two *Sahihs*" (*sahih* means authentic). *Sunans* are hadith collections designed to be used as legal references; they are organised by topic and use only hadiths traced back to the Prophet

Of the two *Sahihs*, al-Bukhari is considered the most authoritative and it provides legal commentary whereas Muslim is considered better organised and easier to use. *Sahih* al-Bukhari is considered the second most important Islamic text after the Quran.

ANNEX 1 gives a fuller list of early hadith collections. Similarly, ANNEX 2 lists works that concern the Quran. ANNEX 3 gives examples of historical works.

~~~~

Chapter 9 – Companion Codices Compared

Introduction

Using what early Islamic literature revealed about variants, Arthur Jeffery put together for each of the 15 Companion codices he identified, a list with comments of variants compared with Uthman's codex. It is important to note he did not use any Companion codices as they were all destroyed or lost in the early days; he was using what other early Muslims reported in the early literature.

The number of variants is large, his lists taking up 350 pages of his *Materials for the History of the Text of the Quran*. [1] He lists 1325 variants for the codex of Ibn Mas'ud, which with Ubayy b. Ka'b's codex makes up the two most well-known and mentioned codices. There are 6236 verses in the Quran so 1325 variants give an average of one variant every 4.7 verses.

Some variants are different vowels with the same consonantal text and some are simply different ways of writing letters or forming words, where a word can sometimes be written as a single word or as two words used together.

The majority of variants concern differences in the consonantal text which lead to different words and expressions, sometimes in the form of synonyms, and in some cases words are added or omitted. Some changes look like explanatory touches for theological reasons though this sometimes works the other way around; it is the Uthman text that has the explanatory touch.

Muslim Reactions

Jeffery observed two kinds of reactions to this exposure of early Quranic variants. Most modern Islamic scholars claimed the Uthman text is perfect and the variants must be the accidental or deliberate corruption of the text. Deliberate tampering was the work of later heretics who wanted to win over others to their heretical views by having those views found in the Qurans of famous Companions.

A few, a very few, scholars admitted that the variants were original but explained them by claiming the Companions in the early days made additions to their copies of the Quran only for their own personal and private information to help their understanding of the text, or put in synonyms for words they did not fully comprehend. However, when they publicly recited their text it was the text as delivered by Muhammad and accurately reproduced in Uthman's Quran. [2]

Scale of the Variants

Jeffery also posed the question of whether we have a reliable measure of the scale of the variants. As mentioned above he was reliant on secondary sources. Regarding individual Companion codices, he wrote *"It is unfortunate that not sufficient has survived to enable us to get a real picture of the text of any one of them. ...."*, and *"Most of the references are to the well-known codices of Ibn Mas'ud and Ubayy b. Ka'b"*. [3]

With the general acceptance of Uthman's version interest in other texts which escaped his orders to destroy them, must have gradually declined and they would eventually have disappeared from circulation. There were also continuing efforts to suppress any variants that survived.

Examples of Suppression

An important example is the case of the famous scholar Ibn Shanabudh (245–328 AH) who was recognised as a great authority on the Quran. In 323 AH he sparked an angry reaction by using readings of Ibn Mas'ud, Ubayy b. Ka'b and others in the public prayer in Baghdad and was called before a special tribunal. This was probably instigated by another famous scholar and rival, Ibn Mujahid, who played a major part in the codification of the accepted readings of the Quran.

Ibn Shanabudh defended his action drawing attention to his wide learning in the readings as well as his extensive travels in search of knowledge in the field. However, he was convicted and punished with seven floggings. Ibn Shanabudh recanted and signed a declaration he would use only the Uthman text of the Quran according to the system worked out by Ibn Mujahid, any deviation being punishable by death. [4]

Another indication of the suppression of unwelcome variants is found in the major work of a later scholar, Abu Hayyan (654–745 AH). When referring to a notorious textual variant in his *Tafsir al-Bahr al-Muhit (The Explanation Ocean; Commentary on the linguistic meanings of the Quran)* he specifically states he does not mention variants that are too far removed from Uthman's standard text. This implies that what we have in many of the secondary sources for the variants is what the authors of those sources found useful in their *tafsir* (interpretation) work and sufficiently close to orthodoxy to be allowed to survive.

Suras

Ibn Mas'ud's Codex

According to most sources, Ibn Mas'ud's codex did not contain Sura 1, the Fatiha, and the last two Suras, 113 and 114, of the Quran, found in Uthman's text. The Fatiha is a form of prayer to Allah and some scholars argue it was not originally part of the Quran as it does not start with the command "Say". The last two are similarly prayer like being incantations of taking refuge with Allah and recited as protection against evil, and they also may not have originally been considered part of the Quran. [5]

Some early Muslim historians suggested that Ibn Mas'ud accepted the suras as revealed by the Prophet and were thus part of the Quran but did not approve of them being included in the written text. [6]

Ubayy b. Ka'b's Codex

The codex of Ubayy b. Ka'b included the suras missing from Ibn Mas'ud's codex but had two additional Suras, 115 and 116, not found in Uthman's standard text and placed between the standard

Suras 103 and 104. According to al-Suyuti, they were also found in the codex of Ibn Abbas. They are like short prayers similar to Sura 1, the *Fatiha,* and not prefaced with the command "Say".

Sura 115 al-Khal: O Allah, we seek your help and ask your forgiveness, and we praise you and we don't disbelieve in you. We separate from and leave who sins against you.

Sura 116 al-Hafd: O Allah we worship you and to you we pray and prostrate and to you we run and hasten to serve you. We hope for your mercy and fear your punishment. Your punishment will surely reach the disbelievers. [al-Suyuti, *al-Itqan,* p154]

Some of the early sources say these are supplications which Muhammad occasionally offered at his morning prayers after the recitation of other suras, and were used by Muslims in Muhammad's time, but there is a debate whether or not they should be considered part of the official Quran. [7]

Sura Order

The order of suras in both Ibn Mas'ud's codex and Ubayy b. Ka'b's codex differed considerably from the order in Uthman's text, and from one another. The early sources provide two lists for each of the Companion codices but they are incomplete and inconsistent. The two lists for Ibn Mas'ud's codex can be combined to give a fuller picture and it shows the arrangement of suras in order of descending length is followed more closely than in Uthman's text. The lists assume the content of each sura was in general that found in the corresponding sura in Uthman's text. [8]

Words and Phrases

2:196

A hadith mentioned in Chapter 4 indicating an alternative for the event that prompted the Uthman collection also reveals two ways of reading verse 2:196 of the Quran.

Yazid b. Mu'awiya was in the mosque in the time of al Walid b. Uqba,
sitting in a group among whom was Hudhayfa. An official called out,
"Those who follow the reading of Abu Musa, go to the corner nearest the
Kinda door. Those who follow Abdullah's [Ibn Mas'ud] reading, go to the
corner nearest Abdullah's [Ibn Mas'ud] house". Their reading of Q 2.196
did not agree. One group read, "Perform the pilgrimage to God". The
others read it "Perform the pilgrimage to the Kaba". Hudhayfa became
very angry, his eyes reddened and he rose, parting his qamis at the waist,
although in the mosque. This was during the reign of Uthman. Hudhayfa
exclaimed, "Will someone go to the Commander of the Faithful, or shall I
go myself? This is what happened in the previous dispensations". [Ibn
Abi Dawud, *Kitab al-Masahif*, p11] [9]

2:238

Verse 2:238 today reads *"Maintain your prayers, particularly the*
middle prayer, and stand before Allah in devoutness".

A tradition given in *al-Muwatta'*, the hadith collection of Malik b.
Anas, says that Aisha, the Prophet's wife, ordered a secretary
writing down the Quran for her to insert *".... and the afternoon*
prayer" after *".... the middle prayer"* as she had heard the Prophet
himself say it that way.

A similar tradition in the same collection has Hafsa, Umar's
daughter and another of Muhammad's wives, also ordering her
scribe to make the same change to her text. That this was her own
codex and not the work inherited from her father, Umar, and used
by Zayd when he was working on Uthman's collection is indicated
by a passage in Ibn Abi Dawud's *Kitab al-Masahif. "... It is written in*
the codex of Hafsa, the widow of the Prophet: 'Observe your prayers,
especially the middle prayer and the afternoon prayer'". [Ibn Abi
Dawud, *Kitab al-Masahif*, p87] [10]

2:275

Verse 2:275 begins with the phrase *"....those who devour usury will*
not stand". According to an early source, Ibn Mas'ud's text had the

same introduction but it added the words *".....on the Day of Resurrection"*. [11]

3:19

The standard verse 3:19 reads *"....religion in God's sight is Islam (the Submission)"*. Jeffery's research shows that instead of "Islam", Ibn Mas'ud used the term *"al-Hanifiyyah"* (the Upright Way). This coincides with another reference to this term said by al-Tirmidhi to have been read by Ubayy b. Ka'b in Sura 98.

There were in Arabia before Muhammad's time and during the early part of his mission, people who had given up the worship of idols and called themselves *hunafa,* meaning those who followed the upright way and rejected false beliefs. It is possible that at the beginning Muhammad used this name for those who followed his teachings and revelations and later changed it to "Islam" to indicate they also submitted totally to Allah who reveals the upright way. [12]

3:39

In the Uthman text verse 3:39 reads *"Then the angels called to him as he stood praying in the sanctuary"*. Jeffery's work shows that Ibn Mas'ud's codex had a completely different reading *"Then Gabriel called to him, 'O Zachariah'"*. When comparing codices such completely different readings are found to be as frequent as synonyms. [13]

5:48

The Uthman text reads *".... and We inscribed therein for them (the Jews)"* in verse 5:48. The Ubayy b. Ka'b text read *"... and Allah sent down therein to the Children of Israel"*. [14]

5:89

Verse 5:89 gives the penalty for breach of oaths. The standard text says *".... fast for three days"*. Ibn Mas'ud's text had *".... fast for three successive days"*. This variant was also found in Ubayy b. Ka'b's text. [al-Tabari, *Tafsir al-Quran* 7.19.11] [15]

6:16

Ibn Mas'ud and Ubayy b. Ka'b again had the same variant which said ".... averted by Allah" rather than simply ".... averted" in verse 6:16 [16]

6:153

The standard text says "Verily this is my path". Ibn Mas'ud's text read "This is the path of Your Lord". [al-Tabari, Tafsir al-Quran 8.60.16] [17]

33:6

Verse 33:6 makes a statement about the relationship between Muhammad's wives and believers. It says "The Prophet is closer to the Believers than their own selves, and his wives are their mothers".

Ibn Mas'ud's text added the phrase "....and he is their father". This variant with the phrases the other way around was also found in the codices of Ubayy b. Ka'b and Ibn Abbas. The extra words are very significant and have theological implications. [al-Tabari, Tafsir al-Quran 21.70.8] [18]

58:4

Verse 58:4 in the Uthman text reads "This is imposed so that you may believe in Allah and in his Apostle. Such are the limits [hudud] set by Allah".

Ibn Mas'ud and Ubayy b. Ka'b are said to have had a strikingly different version.

"This is imposed on you so that you may know that Allah is near to you when you pray, ready to answer when you implore Him. For disbelievers there is a cruel torment!" [19]

61:6

In the Uthman derived standard Quran this verse reports Jesus saying "O Children of Israel! I am the messenger of God to you, confirming what came before me of the Torah and bringing good tidings of a messenger to come after me, whose name is Ahmad."

The Ubayy b. Ka'b version is reported to have Jesus saying "*O Children of Israel! I am the messenger of God to you, and I announce to you a prophet whose community will be the last community and by which God will put a seal on prophets and messengers*".

Ubayy's version has an eschatological message, referring to the "*the last community*". This is not mentioned in the standard version which instead stresses a new prophet with a name not unlike Muhammad. [20]

65:11

The official version of 65:11 reads: "*[Allah has sent] an apostle who proclaims to you the explicit Signs [aya] of Allah, so that he may lead the faithful who do good works from darkness to the light*".

The version attributed to Ibn Mas'ud is:

"*[He is] a Prophet who communicates to you the Scripture that I made descend on him and which contains the stories about the Prophets whom I had sent before him to each people*". [21]

92:3

Another hadith mentions a variant.

Narrated Ibrahim: The companions of Abdullah [Ibn Mas'ud] came to Abu Darda, (and before they arrived at his home), he looked for them and found them. Then he asked them: "Who among you can recite (Quran) as Abdullah recites it?" They replied, "All of us". He asked, "Who among you knows it by heart?" They pointed at Alqama. Then he asked Alqama. "How did you hear Abdullah b. Mas'ud reciting Sura al-Layl (The Night)?" Alqama recited: "By the male and the female". Abu Ad-Darda said, "I testify that I heard the Prophet reciting it likewise, but these people want me to recite it:-- 'And by Him Who created male and female.' but by Allah, I will not follow them". [al-Bukhari, USC-MSA web reference Vol. 6, Book 60, Hadith 468 / Arabic reference. Book 65, Hadith 4944]

103:1-3

The official version has: *"By the Hour of the afternoon! Man is in perdition. Except those who have believed"*.

The version attributed to Ibn Mas'ud has: *"By the Hour of the afternoon! Certainly We have created Man for his perdition. Except those who have believed"*.

And in the one attributed to Ali: *"By the Hour of the afternoon! By the vicissitudes of fate! Man is in perdition, and is so until the end of time"*. [22]

112:1

Here Ibn Mas'ud and Ubayy b. Ka'b omitted the word *"say"*. [23]

~~~~

Chapter 10 – Suras and Verses

Abu Musa – Two Missing Suras

A hadith reports Abu Musa said he had forgotten two suras he
could not find in the Uthman text and remembered only a verse
from each one. He claimed one sura was of the length of Sura 9
(which has 129 verses) and the other was similar to one of the
Musabbihat, a group of suras, 57, 59, 61, 62, and 64, beginning
with the same phrase *"Let everything praise Allah...."* which would
have meant he had forgotten the very large number of about 150
verses which were now not in the Quran. Neither of his
remembered verses is in the standard Uthman text. [1]

*Abu Harb b. Abu al-Aswad reported on the authority of his father that
Abu Musa al-Ashari sent for the reciters of Basra. They came to him and
they were three hundred in number. They recited the Quran and he said:*

*You are the best among the inhabitants of Basra, for you are the
reciters among them. So continue to recite it. (But bear in mind) that
your reciting for a long time may not harden your hearts as were
hardened the hearts of those before you.*

*We used to recite a sura which resembled in length and severity to
(Sura) al-Tawba. [Sura 9] I have, however, forgotten it with the exception
of this which I remember out of it: "If there were two valleys full of riches,
for the son of Adam, he would long for a third valley, and nothing would
fill the stomach of the son of Adam but dust".*

*And we used to recite a sura which resembled one of the suras of
Musabbihat, and I have forgotten it, but remember (this much) out of it:
"Oh people who believe, why do you say that which you do not practise"
and "that is recorded in your necks as a witness (against you) and you
would be asked about it on the Day of Resurrection".* [Muslim 1050,
Book 12, Hadith 156 / Book 5, Hadith 2286]

The Son of Adam and the Greed of Man

There are several hadiths that refer specifically to a verse
concerning the "son of Adam" and the greed of man. The verse is

also quoted as being in Companion codices such as those of Ibn Mas'ud, Ubayy, and Ibn Abbas.

Narrated Ibn Abbas: I heard Allah's Messenger saying, "If the son of Adam had money equal to a valley, then he will wish for another similar to it, for nothing can satisfy the eye of Adam's son except dust. And Allah forgives him who repents to Him". Ibn Abbas said: I do not know whether this saying was quoted from the Quran or not. Ata said, "I heard Ibn Az-Zubair saying this narration while he was on the pulpit". [al-Bukhari 6437, Book 81, Hadith 26 / Vol. 8, Book 76, Hadith 445]

Narrated Sahl b. Sa'd: I heard Ibn Az-Zubair who was on the pulpit at Mecca, delivering a sermon, saying, "O men! The Prophet used to say, 'If the son of Adam were given a valley full of gold, he would love to have a second one; and if he were given the second one, he would love to have a third, for nothing fills the belly of Adam's son except dust. And Allah forgives he who repents to Him.'" Ubayy said, "We considered this as a saying from the Quran till the Sura (beginning with) 'The mutual rivalry for piling up of worldly things diverts you..' (102.1) was revealed". [al-Bukhari 6438, Book 81, Hadith 27 / Vol. 8, Book 76, Hadith 446]

Abu Waqid al-Laithii said, "When the messenger of Allah received the revelation we would come to him and he would teach us what had been revealed. (I came) to him and he said 'It was suddenly communicated to me one day: Verily Allah says, We sent down wealth to maintain prayer and deeds of charity, and if the son of Adam had a valley he would leave it in search for another like it and, if he got another like it, he would press on for a third, and nothing would satisfy the stomach of the son of Adam but dust, yet Allah is relenting towards those who relent.'" [al-Suyuti, al-Itqan, p525]

The verse is thus widely attested lending support to the view it was once part of the Quran.

Al-Suyuti reports another tradition similar to the one in Muslim quoted above, except that in this case Abu Musa is not said to have forgotten it but rather that it had been subsequently abrogated. Abrogation is discussed below. [2]

Stoning

The standard Quran says the punishment for adultery is flogging and makes no mention of stoning. [3]

[Q 24:2] *The adulteress and adulterer should be flogged a hundred lashes each, and no pity for them should deter you from the law of God, if you believe in God and the last day; and the punishment should be witnessed by a body of believers.*

In contrast to this, a number of hadiths make clear the Prophet "according to the book of Allah" ordered stoning as the punishment for adultery.

For Example: *.... I will decide between you according to the Book of Allah. .... And, O Unais, go to this woman in the morning, and if she makes a confession, then stone her. He (the narrator) said: He went to her in the morning and she made a confession. And Allah's Messenger made pronouncement about her and she was stoned to death.* [Muslim, Book 29, Hadith 38 / Book 17, Hadith 4209]

.... He (the Holy Prophet) entrusted [her] child to one of the Muslims and then pronounced punishment. And she was put in a ditch up to her chest and he commanded people and they stoned her. [Muslim, Book 29, Hadith 35 / Book 17, Hadith 4206]

Several other traditions report how Umar remembered a verse in the Quran that gave stoning as the punishment for adultery, but it was no longer in the Quran.

Narrated Ibn Abbas: ..... Umar sat on the pulpit and when the callmakers for the prayer had finished their call, Umar stood up, and having glorified and praised Allah as He deserved, he said, "Now then, I am going to tell you something which (Allah) has written for me to say.

.... Allah sent Muhammad with the Truth and revealed the Holy Book to him, and among what Allah revealed, was the Verse of the Rajam, the stoning of a married person (male and female) who commits illegal sexual intercourse, and we did recite this Verse and understood and memorised it. Allah's Messenger did carry out the punishment of stoning and so did we after him. I am afraid that after a long time has passed, somebody will say, 'By Allah, we do not find the Verse of the Rajam in Allah's Book,' and thus they will go astray by leaving an obligation which Allah has

revealed. And the punishment of the Rajam is to be inflicted to any married person (male and female), who commits illegal sexual intercourse, if the required evidence is available or there is conception or confession". [Part of a very long hadith] [al-Bukhari 6830. Book 86, Hadith 57 / Vol. 8, Book 82, Hadith 817]

Narrated Ibn Abbas: Umar said, "I am afraid that after a long time has passed, people may say, 'We do not find the Verses of the Rajam (stoning to death) in the Holy Book', and consequently they may go astray by leaving an obligation that Allah has revealed. Lo! I confirm that the penalty of Rajam be inflicted on him who commits illegal sexual intercourse, if he is already married and the crime is proved by witnesses or pregnancy or confession". Sufyan added, "I have memorised this narration in this way". Umar added, "Surely Allah's Messenger carried out the penalty of Rajam, and so did we after him".* [al-Bukhari 6829, Book 86, Hadith 56 / Vol. 8, Book 82, Hadith 816]

Another hadith has Umar saying the verse was in Sura 33 (al-Ahzab).

Umar said to me "How many verses are contained in the chapter of al-Ahzab?" I said, "72 or 73 verses". He said it was almost as long as the chapter of the Cow, which contains 287 verses, and in it there was the verse of stoning. [4]

However, Umar could not find anyone else who remembered such a stoning verse in the Quran and thus failed to meet the condition of two witnesses to a verse for it to be included in the text. Later some Companions did recall such a verse and a hadith reported the explanation Aisha, the Prophet's youngest wife, gave for its disappearance. [5]

It was narrated that Aisha said: "The Verse of stoning and of breastfeeding an adult ten times was revealed, and the paper was with me under my pillow. When the Messenger of Allah died, we were preoccupied with his death, and a tame sheep came in and ate it". [Ibn Majah, English reference: Vol. 3, Book 9, Hadith 1944 / Arabic reference: Book 9, Hadith 2020]

Hadiths are classified according to how early hadith experts rated the reliability and trustworthiness of the persons in their *isnads*, that is, their chains of transmission. The classifications are: *sahih* (sound); *hasan* (fair); and *da'if* (weak). This hadith in Ibn Majah's collection is classified as *hasan*.

Sura 33 (al-Ahzab) – Missing Verses

The following hadith which appears in many hadith collections has Ubayy b. Ka'b pose further questions about Sura 33 (al-Ahzab/The Joint Forces)

Narrated Aasim b. Bahdalah, from Zirr, who said: Ubayy b. Ka'b said to me: How long is Sura al-Ahzab [Sura 33] when you read it? Or how many verses do you think it is? I said to him: Seventy-three verses. He said: Only? There was a time when it was as long as Sura al-Baqara [Sura 2], and we read in it: "The old man and the old woman, if they commit zina, then stone them both, a punishment from Allah, and Allah is Almighty, Most Wise". [6]

Sura 2 (al-Baqara/The Cow) is the second and longest sura in the Quran and has 286 verses so this implies that something like 200 verses are missing from the Quran as it is today.

Qurtubi's Quran commentary also mentions a loss of verses from Sura 33 quoting a hadith that records another recollection by Aisha.

Aisha narrates: Sura al-Ahzab contained 200 verses during the lifetime of Prophet[s] but when the Quran was collected we only found the amount that can be found in the present Quran. [7]

Another tradition has Hudhayfa b. al-Yaman saying he found some seventy verses missing in the new official text, verses that he used to recite during the lifetime of the Prophet. [8]

Suckling

The Quran is supposed to have contained a law forbidding marriage between two people who had been breastfed by the same woman more than a certain number of times. *Sahih* Muslim, one of the two most famous hadith collections, has the following: [9]

Aisha (Allah be pleased with, her) reported that it had been revealed in the Holy Quran that ten clear sucklings make the marriage unlawful, then it was abrogated (and substituted) by five sucklings and Allah's

Apostle died and it was before that time (found) in the Holy Quran (and recited by the Muslims). [Muslim 1452a, Book 17, Hadith 30 / Book 8, Hadith 3421]

There is no verse concerning such laws concerning suckling in the Quran today.

Sura 9 (al-Tawba) – Missing Verses

According to traditions reported by al-Suyuti, Sura 9 (al-Tawba/Repentance), which has 129 verses, was originally also the same length as Sura 2 (al-Baqara/The Cow) with 286 verses.

Malik says that several verses from chapter 9 (Sura of Repentance) have been dropped from the beginning. Among them is, "In the name of God the compassionate, the Merciful" because it was proven that the length of Sura of Repentance was equal to the length of the Sura of the Cow. [10]

This implies about 160 verses are missing. There are also reports of Hudhayfa saying Sura 9 in the Uthman Quran was perhaps one-fourth or one-third of what it had been during the time of the Prophet. [11]

More on Missing Material

Missing Verses Mentioned by Umar

A tradition in al-Bukhari and the *sira* of Ibn Ishaq both mention a verse that Umar said used to be recited.

.... And then we used to recite among the Verses in Allah's Book: "O people! Do not claim to be the offspring of other than your fathers, as it is disbelief (unthankfulness) on your part that you claim to be the offspring of other than your real father". [Part of a very long hadith] [al-Bukhari 6830, Book 86, Hadith 57 / Vol. 8, Book 82, Hadith 817]

There are other verses that Umar believed had been dropped or lost from the Quran including one on being dutiful to parents and one on *jihad*. Three other Companions also mention the verse concerning being dutiful to parents. [12]

Other

Anas b. Malik remembered a verse which was revealed when some Muslims were killed in a battle but was later "lifted". [13]

Various reports say that prominent Companions found the official Uthman text missed parts of the revelations that they had themselves heard from the Prophet or found them changed. Ubayy b. Ka'b recited Sura 98 (al-Bayyina/Clear Evidence) as he heard it from the Prophet and included two verses not in the Uthman text. Maslama b. Mukhallad al-Ansari also had two verses not in the Uthman text and Aisha had another. [14]

Views of Early Muslim Scholars

A good many very early Muslim historians are reported to have believed the Quran was not complete much of it being lost before collection. Abdullah b. Umar, the learned son of the caliph Umar, was most emphatic and is recorded as saying:

It is reported from Ismail b. Ibrahim from Ayyub from Naafi from Ibn Umar who said: "Let none of you say 'I have acquired the whole of the Quran'. How does he know what all of it is when much of the Quran has disappeared? Rather let him say 'I have acquired what has survived'". [15]

Abrogation

Missing verses can be explained under the Islamic doctrine of abrogation. From early times the great majority of Muslim scholars have recognised the Quran contains contradictions. A well-known example is the Quran's references to alcohol. One reference is non-judgemental, another is disapproving, another forbids prayer while drunk, and yet another reference calls for total abstention. [16]

While not directly addressing this problem a number of verses in the Quran itself gave early scholars ideas for dealing with it. For example, Q 2:106 says:

Whatever ayah (verse) We abrogate or cause to be forgotten We bring one better; or the like thereof.

Scholars took the view certain commands were only of temporary application and as circumstances changed they were replaced by others, but because the replaced command was the word of God it should still be recited as part of the Quran. This, of course, meant it was vital to know the order in which the contradicting verses were revealed, and much scholarly work went into determining and agreeing on a chronology for the suras.

This form of abrogation – (a) a passage can exist in the Quran but no longer have any legal force because it is abrogated by a later verse – is the most prominent and widely accepted, though over the centuries there has been disagreement over what and how many verses are so abrogated.

There are two other forms of abrogation less well-recognised and both controversial.

(b) Passages that no longer appear in the Quran but still have legal force and are known of through hadiths reporting what the Prophet said. The penalty of stoning for adultery is an example.

(c) Passages absent from the Quran that have been forgotten. According to this form, the Quran does not contain all of what was revealed by Muhammad. Quran verses also support this idea:

Q 87:6-7 *We shall cause you to recite, and you shall not forget Except what God wills...* and Q 13:39 *God will delete or confirm what he will; and with him is the 'mother' of the Book.*

It would take another book to get anywhere near to doing justice to this complicated subject. Two hadiths give contradictory reports of what was done in the early days. One clearly states material was deliberately omitted.

Narrated Ibn Abbas: Umar said, Ubayy was the best of us in the recitation (of the Quran) yet we leave some of what he recites. Ubayy says, "I have taken it from the mouth of Allah's Messenger and will not leave for anything whatever". But Allah said "None of Our Revelations do We abrogate or cause to be forgotten but We substitute something better or similar". [al-Bukhari 5005, Book 66, Hadith 27 / Vol. 6, Book 61, Hadith 527]

Another hadith reports Uthman's determination to include everything even the abrogated.

Narrated Ibn Az-Zubair: I said to Uthman (while he was collecting the Quran) regarding the Verse: "Those of you who die and leave wives ...". This Verse was abrogated by another Verse. So why should you write it? (Or leave it in the Quran)? Uthman said. "O son of my brother! I will not shift anything of it from its place". [al-Bukhari, Book 65, Hadith 4530 / Vol. 6, Book 60, Hadith 53]

~~~~

PART 3

CLOSURE

Chapter 11 – Closure of the Quran

Introduction

Islamic tradition and Islamic and most Western scholarship give Uthman (r. 644–656 CE) the credit for establishing the standard and codified text of the Quran in its consonantal form (*rasm*), the way Arabic was written in his time, lacking in signs for vowels and the use of marks for distinguishing consonants written the same way.

Arabic writing developed in the decades after Uthman and during the rule of caliph Abd al-Malik (r. 685–705 CE) the text of the Quran was given marks for vowels and more and consistent diacritics for uniquely identifying all consonants. It was becoming a *scriptio plena*, a writing system in which all consonants and vowels are consistently represented by characters or markings, enabling the accurate and unambiguous representation of spoken words.

Nevertheless, there is epigraphic and literary evidence and traditions that suggest much more happened concerning the text and codification of the Quran in the post-Uthman decades, especially under caliph Abd al-Malik.

Broadly speaking there are three scenarios. Firstly, Uthman did all the necessary work and was successful. Abd al-Malik's time only saw improvements regarding Arabic writing.

Secondly, Uthman initiated the effort to standardise the Quran but was not successful. Ibn Mas'ud's codex was still in use in Kufa at the end of the seventh century. So for certain it was still necessary to enforce a standard Quran and there is a body of traditions reporting how some 50 years after Uthman, Abd al-Malik's governor of Iraq, al-Hajjaj (g. 694–714 CE)(75–95 AH), worked to standardise the text of the Quran and to ensure the standard was the only version used throughout the Islamic world, what one scholar has referred to as the "Second *Masahif* project". [1]

Thirdly, the uncertainty and continued existence of other texts meant the final redaction and codification of the Quran may have happened only at the end of Abd al-Malik's rule (r. 685–705 CE), three-quarters of a century after the death of the Prophet (632 CE).

The second and third scenarios are aspects of what is sometimes called the "Emergent Canon" model and, in addition to the above, there is the extreme view Uthman played no part and the traditions about his collection are false. [2]

Epigraphy and Written Evidence

The most quoted examples of Quranic variation in epigraphic form are found in two long inscriptions in glass mosaic, encircling the inner and outer faces of the octagonal arcade of the Dome of the Rock. The Dome of the Rock is an Islamic shrine on the Temple Mount in Jerusalem. It was built on the order of Abd al-Malik during the second Muslim Civil War (*Fitna*) and completed in 691–92 CE, some 40 years after Uthman's standardisation. [3]

The two inscriptions number altogether about 750 words and nearly all of what is quoted from the Quran is what is found in the Quran today. The quotes are short, one or two verses, and from different parts of the Quran mostly denying the divinity of Christ, rebuking Trinitarian Christianity, and asserting the prophethood of Muhammad. [4]

The odd aspects concern conflation and a change of person. The inscription says *"Unto Him belongeth sovereignty and unto Him belongeth praise. He quickeneth and He giveth death; and He is Able to do all things"* which is a conflation of a phrase from Q 64:1 and two others from Q 57:2 that appears twice.

The Quranic passage 19:33 *"Peace be upon me, the day I was born, and the day I die, and the day I am raised alive!"* is changed from the first person to the third person, *"Peace be on him the day he was born, and the day he dies, and the day he shall be raised alive!"* There are a few more but very minor variations.

Western scholarship is divided some seeing the variations as very significant. If the Quran had at this time been fully codified and canonised no one would have dared make such amendments to the text, even so few, especially on one of Islam's most sacred and prestigious monuments, and it is odd that there are dozens of passages from different parts of the Quran. It indicates the Quranic text must have still been at least partially fluid at the end of the seventh century. Others believe the changes are simply adaptations, making different texts put together, suitable for a public inscription. The first to third person conversion brings the passage into line with the one before which is in the third person.

Traditions and al-Hajjaj
A number of traditions make clear there was considerable activity concerning how the Quran was written and the enforcement of a standardised version, in the late seventh century long after Uthman's collection and distribution of a standardised Quran.

Ubaydallah b. Ziyad
According to one report Ibn Ziyad (d. 686 CE), the governor of the Basra and Kufa region, added *alfay harfin* to the Quranic text. Though this can be translated as "two thousand letters" assuming a particular context, the phrase also means "two thousand words". It is most likely Ibn Ziyad was implementing an improved script by ensuring a particular vowel letter was always used where needed rather than adding text. [5]

Al-Hajjaj - Work on the Writing and Text
Many reports concern al-Hajjaj (661–714 CE), the governor of Iraq under Abd al-Malik. It is said he instructed one of his scribes to improve the Quranic script by using diacritical marks to distinguish consonants and show vowels. Another version of the report has him, on the orders of Abd al-Malik, instructing two learned Islamic scholars to do this, and to divide the text into equal parts. He is also said to have organised a group of Quran reciters to count the text's consonants, words, and verses, and to divide it into sections of equal length.

Another report suggests al-Hajjaj's interest extended to the words of the text. Ibn Dawud, the author of the Book of Quran Codices discovered in 1937, lists 11 passages where al-Hajjaj changed the Uthman *rasm* mainly by adding or removing letters. [6]

Al-Hajjaj - Enforcement of Standard

According to traditions, al-Hajjaj played a leading role in the acceptance and use of one standard Quran. He not only sent the standard version to the major centres of the Islamic empire, such as Kufu where Ibn Mas'ud's *mushaf* remained in use, as Uthman had done, he also sent copies to smaller towns, and he ruled that the standard codex should be read in mosques on Thursdays and Fridays. There was still some opposition, Abd al-Aziz, the governor of Egypt, rejected the copy sent there and had his own codex produced.

Al-Hajjaj also organised a task force to inspect existing Quran codices and to destroy those that did not agree with the standard. Owners of destroyed copies received compensation of sixty dirhams.

Notwithstanding some suggestion of his work on the text, the best to be gleaned from the traditions is that al-Hajjaj circulated a re-edition of the Uthman text with added diacritical marks, also possibly subdivided into parts of equal length.

These traditions regarding al-Hajjaj's steps to impose a standardised Quran mean Quranic texts with significant variants must have existed and been in use as late as 700. [7]

Sayings of Abd al-Malik and al-Hajjaj

Alfred-Louis de Prémare, a modern Western scholar, who argues for the collection and redaction of the Quran in the post-Uthman period, lists sayings of Abd al-Malik and al-Hajjaj that can be interpreted to mean late collection and redaction was indeed the case.

One report has Abd al-Malik saying he "collected" the Quran during Ramadan, but here the term used could also mean he "memorised" the Quran during this important time. He was not putting it together.

A hadith in *Sahih* Muslim has al-Hajjaj telling his listeners during a sermon to *"Compose the Quran as Gabriel has composed it"*. De Prémare believed the audience was made up of scribes charged with writing the Quran and al-Hajjaj was instructing them how to put the Quran together meaning this had not already been done. However, the context, the giving of a sermon, and the hadith itself indicate this was about the order in which to recite the Quran. [8]

Uthman's Role?

At one extreme in the debate over the closure of the Quran is the argument that the traditions concerning Uthman's role are all false, and it was only under Abd al-Malik that a collection and final redaction was implemented. This view held by the early Western scholar Paul Casanova (1911) has been recently re-energised by Alfred-Louis de Prémare and Stephen Shoemaker.

De Prémare emphasises the strong evidence for the instability of the Quranic text right up to the end of the seventh century, such as the traditions concerning the Quranic interests of Abd al-Malik and al-Hajjaj, and the non-standard aspects of the inscriptions on the Dome of the Rock. De Prémare believes the Uthman collection traditions were propaganda, fabricated to boost the status and dynastic claims of the Umayyad caliphs by assigning to Uthman, the first Umayyad, such a prestigious task. [9]

As discussed above in Chapter 6, a great many of the Uthman collection traditions can be traced back to al-Zuhri as the source, but the question remains was al-Zuhri simply the first or possibly only hadith collector of his time whose transmission survived to pass on the Uthman account or was he the initial fabricator of the account? Al-Zuhri was a young man who worked at the court of Abd al-Malik and lived to 742 CE, 39 years after his rule.

On the other hand, one can pose the question if Abd al-Malik was responsible for both the initial collection and final redaction of the Quran rather than Uthman that for such an important accomplishment there would be traditions that explicitly mentioned it. There are none. This assumes that Islamic traditions would preserve the entire range of what people knew or believed about events at the end of the seventh century and beginning of the eighth.

A fact that does support the view a collection and redaction under Uthman really happened and he ordered the destruction of other codices is the existence in the early literary sources of reports criticising Uthman for doing what he did. It was controversial. There are reports of him defending himself against the accusation of reducing the Quran to a single book and of having "burnt the book of God". There are also reports defending what he did such as a report that Ali gave a speech defending him against the charge of burning codices.

In analysing these various reports, the modern Western scholar, Gregor Schoeler, concludes the controversy was genuine. [10] Uthman did order the collection of the Quran, the enforcement of the standard version, and destruction of other codices. It is most unlikely that any fabricators of a tradition describing Uthman's enforcement of the standard text of the Quran would at the same time also have produced accounts defending him against accusations which had not yet been voiced.

Historical Likelihood

In examining how the Quran came to be codified and a single standard version accepted and used by all believers it is relevant to consider the historical circumstances; the standing and power of the leaders, how they ruled, and what they achieved.

Chase Robinson in his book, *Abd al-Malik (Makers of the Muslim World)*, provides a comparison of these factors for Uthman and Abd al-Malik. [11] Uthman's rule (r. 644–656) was contentious. There was public opposition to his policies and armed revolts and his rule ended with his assassination. There are few signs of the projection of authority and power such the minting of coins, public buildings and inscriptions, and it is difficult to envisage the imposition of a single version of the Quran under Uthman.

Abd al-Malik ruled for longer (r. 685–705). His rule also faced opposition at the beginning, large parts of the Islamic empire being ruled by rivals, but he prevailed. He is notable for the introduction of Islamic currency and at first, though the image was later changed, it depicted the caliph as the spiritual leader of the Muslim community as well as its supreme military commander. He also ordered the use of Arabic as the official language of government throughout the Islamic empire where many languages were spoken.

And, of course, he was responsible for the construction of the Dome of the Rock. Abd al-Malik *"had the resources to attempt such a redaction and to impose the resulting text"*, and he made the effort to Islamicise political authority *"by broadcasting ideas of order and obedience in a distinctly Islamic idiom"*. Robinson concludes that *"instead of speaking of an Uthmanic text, we should probably speak of a Marwanid one"*. (Abd al-Malik was of the Marwanid branch of the Umayyads.)

This very positive picture of Abd al-Malik certainly makes it look more likely that it was under his rule that a single version of the Quran came into force, but it does not rule out that Uthman played an important initial role, and was responsible for most of the basic *rasm* if not all of it.

Non-Muslim Sources and Late Closure

In the absence of contemporary Islamic accounts, Western scholars have made use of Christian writings from those early times to help explain the history of the Quran.

Three sources, a dialogue between Patriarch John of Antioch (r. 631–648 CE) and a Muslim commander, an anonymous non-Muslim chronicler writing around the year 680 CE, and the chronicle of John Bar Penkaye (probably written 687–8 CE), discuss religious matters, such as the denial of the divinity of Christ according to Islamic teaching, the importance of the Kaba,

82

and treatment of non-Muslims, but there is no mention of the Quran.

Two other sources, a debate between a Monk of Bet Hale and an Arab notable, and the chapter about Islam in John of Damascus' history (d. c. 750 CE), refer to a Muslim book and the teachings of Muhammad but mention several works, Sura 2 being referred to as if it was a separate work. Interesting though these accounts are, they are countered by the existence of early Quranic manuscripts [See Chapter 14] and, in any case, can be easily explained.

Two other Christian sources though both very controversial and open to challenge address head-on the closure of the Quran, suggesting it was not until the end of the 7th century CE. [12]

Leo III

An eight century Armenian chronicler, Lewond, cites a letter that the Byzantine Emperor Leo III (r. 717–741 CE) wrote to the caliph Umar II (r. 717–720 CE) in response to an invitation from the caliph to become a Muslim. Leo responds with arguments for the truth of Christianity and an outright attack on the truth of the Quran.

As for your (book), you have already given us examples of such falsifications, and one knows, among others, of a certain Hajjaj, named by you as Governor of Persia, who had men gather up your ancient books, which he replaced by others composed by himself, according to his taste, and which he propagated everywhere in your nation, because it was easier by far to undertake such a task among a people speaking a single language. From this destruction, nevertheless, there escaped a few of the works of Abu Turab, for Hajjaj could not make them disappear completely.

Al-Kindi

About 100 years later another critique of the Quran is made by Abd al-Masih b. Ishaq al-Kindi, an Arab Christian who worked at the court of the caliph al-Ma'mun (r. 813–833 CE). In correspondence with a friend al-Kindi argues against the Islamic objections and refutations of Christianity. He switches to a polemic against Islam. He is obviously well-informed regarding the various traditions about the collection of the Quran and says the following:

Then followed the business of Hajjaj b. Yusuf, who gathered together every single copy he could lay hold of, and caused to be omitted from the text a great many passages. Amongst these, they say, were verses revealed concerning the House of Umayyad with the names of certain persons, and concerning the House of Abbas also with names. Six copies of the text thus revised were distributed to Egypt, Syria, Medina, Mecca, Kufa and Basra. After that he called in and destroyed all the preceding copies, even as Uthman had done before him.

.... an evidence that many different hands have been at work therein, and caused discrepancies, adding to the text, or cutting out there from whatever they liked or disliked.

.... All that I have said is drawn from your own authorities; and no single argument has been advanced but what is based on evidence accepted by yourselves.

That two quite independent Christian texts, as well as some Muslim traditions, claim al-Hajjaj had a significant hand in finalising the text of the Quran circa 700 CE support that is what happened.

~~~

Chapter 12 – Indications in the Quran

This chapter looks at the characteristics and features of the Quran itself to see if there are any indications of when the text became fixed especially whether or not it remained fluid after Uthman's collection and subject to insertions and alterations.

No Indication of Events or Issues Post-Muhammad: from 632 to 700

It is not unreasonable to think the scholars who put together the final version of the Quran might have been required by those in-charge, or themselves tempted, to make additions or changes to the text of the Quran to reflect contemporary concerns and issues.

The other great body of Islamic sacred text, the hadiths, has many examples of content that shows hadiths were changed or created well after their supposed origin. [1] There are hadiths where the Prophet comments on events or issues in the Muslim world that only came about after his lifetime that he could never have known about. Such anachronistic hadiths concerning conflicts and matters after the Prophet's death cannot be his words. Albeit, some Muslim scholars claimed he could see the future!

The modern Western scholar Fred Donner has examined the Quran in this regard and he observes:

.... *we find not a single reference to events, personalities, groups or issues that clearly belong to periods after the time of Muhammad - Abbasids, Umayyads, Zubayrids, Alids, the dispute over free will, the dispute over tax revenues and conversion, tribal rivalries, conquests etc.*

If the text of the Quran was being edited, changed or added to, up to c. 700 CE, it is remarkable that it does not touch on or hint at, directly or indirectly, the major issues of Islamic development between the death of the Prophet in 632 CE and c. 700 CE the time of the enforcement of a standard text. Donner takes this to mean the Quran was put together very shortly after Muhammad's death and the text, at least in *rasm* form, closed before the first major development, the First Civil war (656–661 CE). [2]

The Significance or Otherwise of Anachronisms

Difference Between the Quran and the Hadith

Another modern Western scholar, Stephen Shoemaker, argues the absence of anachronisms does not fix the text of the Quran to the time before major historical events such as the First Civil war and in response to Donner's observation he says:

.... the Quran's lack of anachronisms can be largely explained by the Quran's focus primarily on the timeless message of a prophetic past and a present defined especially by inter-religious conflicts, the need for community order, and an impending doom that will soon bring history to a close.

The contents of the Quran largely concern the restoration of an ancient faith that had been practised by Abraham and Moses, and it was being revealed again to humanity. The Quran avoids references to any aspect of the current historical environment. The only points of time that figure in the Quran are the Creation and the Last Judgement which is imminent, and it is mainly concerned with the overriding need for mankind to choose between good and evil before judgement day. In this context, it is not surprising there are no forged predictions concerning future issues. [3]

In contrast, hadiths cover a vast range of subjects, from everyday matters, personal hygiene, how to pray, food and clothing, to religious policy, political matters, and current events. Al-Bukhari's famous collection covers 97 topics, and one the most popular being military campaigns and *jihad* (12% of hadiths). Hadiths thus provide enormously more scope and opportunity for anachronistic fabrications. [4]

It would be far easier to insert new or different accounts into traditions on a wide range of subjects created by numerous Companions and transmitted word of mouth, than into the recitation of the Quran, the words of which were widely known and existed in writing.

Example of the Gospel of St John

Shoemaker also notes if the absence of anachronisms in an account means the date of closure, the finalisation of its text, must be at the end of or just after the period covered by that account, the Gospel of St John must have been written and fixed very soon after the death of Jesus, c. 32 CE. Yet, as far as is known, no New Testament scholar has drawn such a conclusion and the great majority believe it was the last gospel written and its text was finalised c. 100 CE, nearly 70 years after the life of Jesus. Thus, the absence of anachronisms in a text *"cannot be used to date it close to the events that it purports to describe or to verify its authenticity"*. [5]

There may, however, be some anachronisms in this gospel. Nicolai Sinai, in his paper, *When did the consonantal skeleton of the Quran reach closure?* published in 2014, [6] gives the example of the statement in the gospel *"the Jews had already agreed that anyone who confessed Jesus to be the Messiah would be put out of the synagogue"*. [John 9:22]

He explains a leading New Testament scholar, Bart Ehrman, has said that during Jesus' lifetime there was no Jewish official policy against accepting Jesus as the Messiah, whereas towards the end of the first century some synagogues began to exclude members who believed in Jesus' messiahship.

Possible Quranic Anachronism

Shoemaker mentions what could be an anachronism in the Quran. [7] The Quran gives its version of the Nativity of Jesus (Q 19:16-33) that suggests it was written after the conquest of Palestine, and thus after Muhammad's death. It makes use of traditions that link to a Christian pilgrimage sanctuary, the church or seat, of the "God-Bearer" Mary, located between Jerusalem and Bethlehem. It is clear the Muslim conquerors attached significant importance to this church as they turned it into a mosque and copied its design in the construction of the Dome of the Rock.

Sinai explains the Quran's account of the Nativity has some relationship to this pilgrimage sanctuary and this could be the result of its obvious importance to the Muslim conquerors of

Palestine. It is even possible that all of Sura 19 originated after the conquest of Palestine. [8]

There is though, still the possibility that traditions concerning the sanctuary spread before the Palestinian conquest and were known where and when the Quran was first being revealed.

Other Features

Sinai's paper provides a comprehensive and balanced summary of the evidence and arguments for and against the early closure of the Quran's text as covered above and in support of early closure he mentions the following further points. [9]

Nothing on the Occasions of Revelations

In places the Quran is very hard to understand, it needs interpretation. For this exegesis, or *tafsir* in Arabic, early Muslim scholars looked to the circumstances of a revelation; what was the Prophet doing, what was happening when he received the revelation, what was the occasion of the revelation. The Quran itself is equally uninformative in this respect and scholars had only the large and growing body of traditions about Muhammad's doings and sayings to turn to, which came to form the *sira*, the biography of the Prophet.

The meaning of, or the way to interpret, a Quranic passage often becomes clear when it is seen as part of a tradition concerning what Muhammad was doing or saying, or what was happening to him. Such traditions assumed enormous importance. It is even possible that the reverse happened, traditions were created to explain Quranic passages (this deserves a whole new chapter, even a book! and will not be expanded on here!).

In any event, given the vital role played by occasions of revelations and the importance of the correct interpretation of the Quran in the lives of Muslims, it is noticeable and surprising that no such information crept into the Quran if it was being added to or modified by post-Muhammad redactors. There are not even any minor hints or references to what was happening to Muhammad or what he was doing. This is most easily explained by the text of the Quran being fixed by the middle of the seventh century (c. 650 CE) or earlier.

Though again, the argument can be made that the Quran's editors in the time of the Marwanid Umayyad caliphs (684–750 CE) or before would be very careful not to change the unique character of the Quran described above and as a collection of God-given revelations.

No Corrections

The Quranic text has a number of grammatical and spelling oddities, or "rough edges" as Sinai describes them. There are five examples of incorrect case agreement and the mystery of the spelling of Mecca. The Quran refers to a place called Bakka which nearly everyone takes to be Mecca. These rough edges which could easily be corrected, and without any great fuss, indicate the text was firmly fixed rapidly after Muhammad's death, no one willing to make any changes without his involvement.

Possible Additions

Various other factors can be examined that might indicate how and when a passage became part of the Quran. This section gives some examples of such work by modern Western scholars.

Zayd

David Powers, in his book *Muhammad Is Not the Father of Any of Your Men: The Making of the Last Prophet* (2009), [10] argues the verses Q 33:36-40 are a later insertion in the Quran. One of these verses gives Muhammad permission to marry the divorced wife of his adopted son, Zayd. Marrying a divorced daughter-in-law was forbidden and the Quran now creates a distinction between the wives of natural sons and the wives of adopted sons.

Verse 37. *[Recall] when you said to the one on whom God and you yourself have bestowed favour, "Keep your wife to yourself and fear God", and you hid within yourself what God would reveal, and you feared the people when God had better right to be feared by you. When Zayd had finished with her, We gave her to you in marriage, so that there should be no difficulty for the believers concerning the wives of their adopted sons, when they have finished with them. God's command was fulfilled.*

And verse 40, says:

Verse 40. *Muhammad is not the father of any of your men, but the messenger of God and the seal of Prophets. God is aware of everything.*

Powers believes even if Zayd was a real person and the adopted son of Muhammad, traditions about him were fabricated and involved the insertion of the above verses. The set of which they are part can easily be removed from the Quran without leaving an obvious gap, and it is also remarkable that the only person mentioned by name in the whole of the Quran, other than Muhammed who is mentioned three times, is Zayd.

In a further book, *Zayd*, published in 2014, [11] Powers analyses the many traditions relating to Zayd and argues they are modelled on biblical narratives about earlier characters in Abrahamic scripture, which strongly suggests they are not genuine accounts of what the man called Zayd did at the time of the Prophet.

The motive for fabrication lay in two Islamic beliefs that came to the fore after Muhammad died. Muhammad was the "seal of the prophets", he was the last prophet, and Prophecy remained in the same family and passed from father to son. The idea that Muhammad was the last prophet was particularly important as it meant Islam superseded Judaism and Christianity. Prophecy passing down a family line is well established in Abrahamic religions. It was thus vital to eliminate Zayd as a potential heir.

Tradition also reports that just after Zayd divorced his wife and before Muhammad's marriage to her, the Prophet told Zayd, *"I am not your father"*, to counter public concern about his marriage to a daughter-in-law.

And soon after this, adoption was abolished. The Quran hints at this. Q 33:4-5 says *"God has not .... made your adopted sons your [real] sons .... Call them after their fathers"*, but early Muslim jurists based the abolition on a report that the Prophet said anyone who claims as his father someone other than his biological father, or claims as his son someone other than his biological son, is an infidel who will be denied entrance to paradise.

Powers also says the insertion of Q 33:37, quoted above, also meant two other changes had to be and were made in the Quran.

Q 33:6 originally read *"The prophet is closer to the believers than they are themselves, he is their father and his wives are their mothers"*. The standard version of the Quran does not have the phrase *"he is their father"*. [See Chapter 9, Companion Codices Compared, which mentions the phrase *"he is their father"* was reported in no-longer extant Companion codices.]

Q 4:23, which prohibited marriage with *"your daughters-in-law"* was changed so instead of referring to daughters-in-law it read, *"the wives of your sons who are from your own loins"*.

Powers provides further background and arguments on a number of these points especially the contemporary historical events that played a big part in Muhammad becoming the "Seal of the Prophets" in his paper *Sinless, Sonless and Seal of Prophets: Muhammad and Quran 33:36-40, Revisited*, published in 2020. [12]

Q 3:7

Another example is provided by Nicolai Sinai. His book, *The Quran: A Historical-Critical Introduction* (2017), [13] describes the strong evidence that the Quran was composed before the Arab expansion and that it is in line with the traditional account of Muhammad's historical and political career but this does not rule out post-prophetic insertions.

He mentions Q 3:7 as such a possibility. The verse states that what has been sent down to the Messenger contains verses that are "firm" or "clear" and others that "resemble one another" in this instance meaning they are ambiguous. It condemns those who follow what is ambiguous, thus seeking temptation and its interpretation.

This recognition that in places the Quran is ambiguous is in striking contrast to the many verses that extol the Quran's clarity;

Q 12:1, 26:2, and 43:2, for example. And verses Q 75:16-19 state that God himself will see to the clarity of the revelations.

Sinai explains it is possible the emerging Islamic community soon after Muhammad's death found itself in a difficult situation. Revelations had been "cut-off". There would be no more, no growth, and no revision, and some of what they already had contained considerable ambiguity.

In these circumstances, Q 3:7 was inserted to deal with this ambiguity. It discourages believers from paying attention to unclear or puzzling passages in the Quran and urges them to concentrate on what is clear and easily intelligible. Another indication of later insertion is the sequence Q 3:7-9 can be removed from the text without creating an obvious gap. Verse 6 links up with verse 10. Verse 7 also uses terms used elsewhere in the Quran but with semantic shifts.

Sinai notes that even if verses 7-9 are a later addition, this does not mean they postdate Muhammad.

The Romans Will Win
This refers to a prophecy in Q 30:2-7. The verses report the Romans in a conflict against an unknown enemy in which they are vanquished but predict the Romans will eventually be victorious and on that day the Believers will rejoice.

Tommaso Tesei [14] shows when the opening verse is read according to a particular Islamic reading the verses closely parallel other 7th century CE prophecies in non-Muslim sources concerning a Roman defeat by the Sasanians followed by a Roman victory. Q 30:2-7 is referring to the conflict between the Byzantines (the Romans) and Sasanians that lasted for about thirty years at the start of the 7th century (602–628 CE).

He notes these prophecies are of a form often found in apocalyptic texts. The technical term is *vaticinium ex eventu* which means the author already had the information about the events being "foretold". The text is written after the event but is worded so as to appear the prophecy took place before the event.

Thus, it could only have been after Heraclius, Byzantine Emperor, was victorious and signed the peace treaty in 628 CE ending the conflict that the various prophecies on the Byzantine-Sasanian war—including the prophecy in the Quran—could have been composed.

Tesei also argues that the prophecy became known to the emerging Muslim community during the first Arab raids into Palestine a few years after 628 CE when it encountered Arab speakers who had been living under Byzantine jurisdiction

That the Believers should rejoice at a Roman victory lies in the fact that the prophecy is eschatological concerning a temporal moment of sacred history. The Byzantine Empire had acquired the reputation that it would be the last world power before the Eschaton (the last day before the end of time) and thus having proved itself the world power, to the Believers, the day of Judgement was closer.

~~~~

Chapter 13 – Canonical Variant Readings

The Continuing Problem

Traditions and modern scholarship credit al-Hajjaj when he was governor of Iraq during the rule of Abd al-Malik (r. 685–705 CE) with the introduction of vowel signs and the greater use of dots for distinguishing consonant signs as well as the final standardisation of the *rasm*, the consonantal form of the Quran, but manuscripts from the early centuries of Islam show the use of diacritical marks happened slowly and in different ways. [1] The introduction of an agreed writing system that took account of all requirements was bound to be complex and take time. The move from a *scriptio defectiva* to a *scriptio plena* did not happen quickly or evenly.

Further Muslim traditions on the introduction of an improved script vary widely and cannot be relied on and whatever al-Hajjaj did, he did not completely solve the problem of variant readings. Different readings continued and arose, even mixing Uthman and non-Uthman ones, well into Abbasid times (750+ CE)

Ibn Mujahid's Work

The confusion and diversity were finally brought under control some 200 years after al-Hajjaj, and some 250 years after Uthman, by the traditions scholar and Quran reader Ibn Mujahid (859–936 CE) who wrote a book entitled *The Seven Readings*. He concluded that of all the existing readings only those of seven 8th century CE scholars were valid and thereby canonical. [2]

They were all based on a fairly uniform consonantal text and were the prevailing readings, one each in the major Muslim centres of Medina, Mecca, Damascus, and Basra, and three in Kufa. He realised it was impossible to obtain the absolute uniformity which some scholars hoped to achieve.

Ibn Mujahid himself had only the authority of a renowned scholar but he had the support of the vizier, Ibn Muqla, who decreed punishments for anyone who persisted in reciting other readings, and his conclusions were quickly put into effect by the Islamic authorities. It has recently been argued that Ibn Mujahid's selection of readings was driven more by political and practical considerations, such that the main urban centres were all given a voice, rather than by their historical credentials.

In 934 CE, Ibn Miqsam, a leading scholar who believed he could use any reading of the *rasm*, the consonantal outline, that was grammatically correct and made sense, was forced to renounce his view. [3] And, in another famous case, the next year, Ibn Shanabudh, who thought it correct to still use the readings of Ibn Mas'ud and Ubayy b. Ka'b in public prayer and for commenting on and explaining the Quran was similarly condemned, forced to retract his view, and flogged. [4]

Particular methods of reading in Islam are known as *qiraat*. The seven readings, *qiraat*, selected by Ibn Mujahid are listed below in Table 2. In each case, a generation or two later, the versions of two early transmitters of the reading came to be recognised as authoritative, and these are also listed. [5]

Table 2 – Seven Readings Selected by Ibn Mujahid

District	Reader	First Rawi	Second Rawi
Medina	Nafi' (d.785 CE)	Warsh (812)	Qalun (835)
Mecca	Ibn Kathir (737)	al-Bazzi (854)	Qunbul (903)
Damascus	Ibn Amr (736)	Hisham (859)	Ibn Dhakwan (856)
Basra	Abu Amr (770)	ad-Duri (860)	as-Susi (874)
Kufa	Asim (744)	Hafs (805)	Shuba (809)
Kufa	Hamza (772)	Khalaf (843)	Khallad (835)
Kufa	al-Kisai (804)	ad-Duri (860)	Abu l Harith (854)

Despite this big step forward the restriction to seven readings was not welcomed by all and Islamic scholars of different schools and communities continued to discuss and debate what was correct and the list of seven was expanded to 10 and then 14, each also becoming canonical. Eventually, the desire for conformity led to the majority of these transmissions falling into disuse.

Today, there are only two in general use: the Warsh transmission of Nafi's reading which has a long association with the Maliki school of law, and is followed in parts of Africa other than Egypt; and the Hafs transmission of the Asim reading, which has become by a long way the most widely accepted.

The Prophet's *Sabiti Ahruf* and the Canonical Readings

Some modern Muslims and scholars believe Ibn Mujahid's seven readings are based on or related to the *sabiti ahruf*, the seven ways in which the Prophet is reported to have said the Quran could be recited. [6] For example, [See Chapter 5, Variants] a hadith reports:

.... The Quran has been revealed in seven different ways, so recite it in the way that is easier for you. [al-Bukhari 2419. Book 44, Hadith 9 / Vol. 3, Book 41, Hadith 601]

In two papers, Christopher Melchert [7] explains why this is most unlikely. In contrast to modern Muslim scholarship, early Muslim scholars appear to be unanimous that there was no link between the Ibn Mujahid's seven and the *sabati ahruf*. One such famous scholar explained that Ibn Mujahid thought his seven corresponded to the seven written copies Uthman sent to the main Islamic centres. Early scholars before and after Ibn Mujahid wrote about six, eight, ten and other numbers of acceptable readings. And, after Ibn Mujahid, his seven was officially expanded to become ten and even fourteen readings indicating the number seven was not special. Yasin Dutton also discusses this question [8] and points out one of the readings that Ibn Mujahid selected was the result of the merging of earlier locally accepted readings indicating that even if the readings were from a particular place there was diversity in that locality.

It also seems likely that if Ibn Mujahid had believed his selection related to the seven mentioned in earlier Muslim tradition he would have stated this. All the evidence points to the seven canonical readings springing from Uthman's recension.

The Cairo Quran

In 1924 the Hafs-Asim version was adopted by the Egyptian government. It was prompted to do this because they found the Qurans they were importing for state schools had errors and variations. The government destroyed a large number of such texts by sinking them in the Nile River and issued its own text. This Cairo version met with great success and is now seen by the great majority of Muslims and non-Muslims as the official text of the Quran. [9]

The Hafs-Asim version was one of a popular number of readings and thus the Cairo Quran is the result of this selection and not an examination of early manuscripts.

Examples of *Qiraat* Variants

The differences are more than those concerning pronunciation or dialects or spelling. They concern words and grammar and though there is no change in the Quran's teachings, they can change the meaning of particular phrases. Here are a few examples. [10]

Table 3 – Examples of *Qiraat* Variants

Quranic verse	Hafs Reading	Warsh Reading
2:140	… you (plural) say…	… they say…
18:86	… sun sets in a muddy spring …	… sun sets in a warm spring …
21:4	He (Muhammad) said, "My Lord knows …"	Say: My lord knows …
43:19	… they are slaves of the Most Gracious …	… they are with the Most Gracious …
57:24	Allah is the self-sufficient …	Allah, the self-sufficient …

| 66:12 | ... her lord and his books. | ... her lord and his book. |

There are approximately 1300 small differences between these two Qurans.

~~~~

PART 4

EARLY MANUSCRIPTS

Chapter 14 – Extant Early Manuscripts

This chapter gives an introduction to the early Quran manuscripts that we still have today and the methods used for examining what such ancient manuscripts can tell us about the history of the Quran. The following chapters summarise recent work on early Quran manuscripts and the results and findings to date.

A Critical Edition

An important motive for identifying and studying early manuscripts of an ancient work is the wish to create a "critical edition".

A critical edition of a particular work notes in the body of the text where they occur the variants of words, phrases, and other text features, giving the variant and its source. The technical term for this is a *critical apparatus* and there is a recognised standard format for the additional information. Though critical editions exist for some sacred books (e.g., the New Testament) and ancient works of literature (e.g., the Iliad) none has been produced for the Quran. [1]

The first effort to produce a modern critical edition of the Quran was undertaken by Gotthelf Bergsträsser, a Professor of Semitic languages in Munich, and Arthur Jeffery, an Australian, who was at the time a professor at the American University in Cairo. [2] [Jeffery's famous work *Materials for the History of the Text of the Quran* is discussed in Chapter 8, Early Muslim Literature.]

Bergsträsser was also in Cairo and the two worked together studying *qiraat* literature and filming early Quranic manuscripts and in 1926 they agreed to collaborate in preparing an archive of materials and a text of the Quran with a *critical apparatus*. Their plan was likely inspired, at least partly, by the Egyptian governments production and publication of the 1924 Cairo standard edition of the Quran.

Their project suffered a blow when Bergsträsser died in 1933 in an accident while hiking in the Bavarian Alps. The project was continued by Dr. Otto Pretzl, Bergsträsser's successor in Munich and Jeffery reports in his *Materials for the History of the Text of the Quran*, published in 1937:

.... Dr. Pretzl, Bergsträsser's successor at Munich, has begun to organise the Archive for the Korankomission set up by the Bavarian Academy at Bergsträsser's initiation, and has already assembled a goodly collection of photographs of early Kufic Codices and early unpublished qiraat works.

Unfortunately, World War II now dramatically changed the situation and the project was suspended. Pretzl had to join the military and in 1941 he was killed in a plane crash. After the war, Pretzl's position at Munich was filled by Anton Spitaler and on information probably supplied by Spitaler, Jeffery wrote the following.

.... the whole of the Archive at Munich was destroyed by bomb action and by fire, so that the whole of that gigantic task has to be started over again from the beginning. It is thus extremely doubtful if our generation will see the completion of a really critical edition of the Quran.

Then, half a century later this story takes an amazing turn. Spitalar revealed shortly before his death that the archive had not been destroyed but had been in his keeping all that time. Why Spitaler should perpetrate such deception and for so long is not clear and various opinions have been offered but he handed the archive to his former student, Professor Angelika Neuwirth, and it is now an important part of the *Corpus Coranicum Project* which takes up the task initiated by Bergsträsser and Jeffery almost a century ago!

Corpus Coranicum

The Corpus Coranicum is a project of the Berlin-Brandenburg Academy of Sciences and Humanities in Berlin and Potsdam which began in 2007 after Angelika Neuwirth, Professor of Semitic and Arabic studies at the Free University of Berlin, obtained funding. It is a long-term project and is currently funded until 2025. [3]

The project provides free and open access to four databases dealing with the Quranic text and its history:

Quranic Manuscripts (Manuscripta Coranica)
Variant Readings (Variae Lectiones Coranicae)
Texts from the Environment of the Quran (TEQ)
and "Commentary".

The Quranic Manuscripts database connects to 74 libraries all over the world, the Middle East, Far East, Europe and North America, and provides information and images relating to 300, but incomplete, pre-750 manuscripts of the Quran. 2000 folios are covered. A complete Quran might take up about 130 folios so the material available amounts very roughly to the equivalent of 15 complete Qurans.

The work shows how the study of manuscripts and variant literature can reveal the history of the Quranic text and lead to a critical edition reflecting the text's original form.

At a broad level, the project aims to show the development of the first Islamic community especially in terms of the interaction between the Prophet and his audience in Mecca and Medina. It provides a reconstruction of the historical milieu in which the Quran was revealed and shows how it was connected with Late Antiquity and even Europe.

What Exists

There are no complete Qurans that can be dated to the first two centuries AH and the manuscripts and fragments available from this early period do not cover the full Quran of 114 suras found today. The latter suras 77–114 are not found at all, suras 71–76 in only one manuscript, and there is sparse coverage of suras 45–70. [4]

It is very difficult to quantify what exists as the ancient material in its different forms, fragments of folios, individual folios, combined folios, dated and undated material, can be stored and catalogued in different ways.

Some indication is given by the Corpus Coranicum online database of Quranic Manuscripts mentioned above. François Déroche in his book *Qurans of the Umayyads* provides an index of nearly one hundred manuscripts that he identified for his book. Another very useful source is a paper by Sergio Noja-Noseda [5] which has a list of the contents of the known Hijazi manuscripts in the United States, European collections, the Middle East, and Istanbul.

Uthman Manuscripts

It has been claimed that several extant ancient Quranic manuscripts found in a number of museums date back to the time of Uthman. They are contemporary copies of Uthman's famous standard Quran distributed by him during his rule, 644–656 CE, or even one of the copies he distributed. Recent Muslim and Western scholarship, however, concludes none of these copies is an Uthman copy and they come from a later time. [6]

Given that Uthman, according to tradition, did so much to establish the standard text produced on his orders, sending copies to the main centres of Islam and ordering the destruction of all other versions, it is surprising there is no extant recognised copy of what he distributed.

The two most famous manuscripts that claim to be Uthman copies are the Topkapi manuscript in Istanbul and the Samarqand manuscript in Uzbekistan. These have been studied by Dr. Tayyar Altikulaç, a leading Turkish scholar. The Topkapi manuscript has decorative illuminations, and such illumination work was not practised at the time of Uthman. It also makes some use of diacritic dots or vowel marks, another later development. [7]

Regarding the Samarqand manuscript, Altikulaç gives six reasons, *"almost no discipline of spelling, different ways of writing the same word, scribal mistakes, copyists' mistakes, written by a scribe who had no writing experience, and later added signs after verses"*.

He concludes, "....*we can say that the [Samarqand] Mushaf was neither the Mushaf which Caliph Uthman was reading when he was martyred, nor any one of the Mushafs that he sent to various centers . . . nor the copy that was kept in Medina for the benefit of the people*".[8]

Both the Topkapi and Samarqand manuscripts are written in the Kufic script. Uthman's text produced in Medina would have been written in the Hijazi script, from the Hijaz, as noted above, the region in which Medina is located. The Kufic script originated and came into regular use in Kufa in modern Iraq and only came into wide use throughout the Muslim lands well after Uthman's death.

Similar problems and anachronisms can be found with the other manuscripts that claim to be Uthman copies.

Vital Tools

Dating

The date of an ancient manuscript, the date it was produced, is of paramount importance. Even though the manuscript might obviously be old, without this knowledge we can't determine what the manuscript tells us about the environment or circumstances in which it was produced and we can't apply what we might know about a particular time to the manuscript.

Later Quran manuscripts include colophons. A colophon is where the scribe or copyist who created the manuscript records his name, location, date of the work, who he is working for, and other related information. It is generally found at the end of a manuscript. None of the surviving material from the first centuries has a genuine colophon. [9]

There are methods for dating ancient manuscripts that all depend on a great degree of human judgement and expertise. [10]

The first concerns the study of ancient writing (palaeography). Early manuscripts are usually written in the Arabic Hijazi script, that is, from Hijaz, the region of northwest Arabia where Mecca and Medina are located and were written without diacritic marks or with very few. Considerable care is needed in using this method as scribes can change what they do over time and according to their region. The defining features of Hijazi script are not necessarily static. Word spelling (orthography) also developed over time and can indicate when a script was written.

Another method involves the study of the manuscript materials used, writing layout, and codex construction (codicology). [See Chapter 3 for a definition of codex.] This can cover the use of vertical or horizontal page formats, page dimensions, number of lines of writing per page, how chapters and verses are divided, inks used, the use of illuminations or other graphic elements and their characteristics, and the use of margins, for example.

The study of language (philology) also plays a part in dating ancient manuscripts.

In recent years, the scientific method of radiocarbon dating has been used but because the method has been known to give misleading results its findings need to be checked against other dating methods. Chapter 17 covers the method in more detail and the results achieved with radiocarbon dating.

Textual Criticism
Textual criticism is a tool for understanding the early history of ancient texts. It is not concerned with the interpretation or the meaning of the content. This is the time before printing and copies of texts were produced by scribes laboriously copying out new copies one at a time by hand. There was wide scope for errors and modifications and the writing system itself was evolving.

Textual criticism involves the comparison of the texts in the different ancient manuscripts for a particular work to determine the earliest or original form of the text and its transmission history. A comparison and analysis of the text differences produce the equivalent of a family tree.

In this regard, it is helpful to have a model or framework for the forms and stages a book might undergo in ancient times before printing when every single book had to be written out by hand. [11]

1 What the author himself wrote, or what he said, or dictated.

2 Copies of this that acquire a degree of authority in particular places or areas; e.g., Companion codices.

3 A canonical text that has authority over a very wide geographical area; e.g., Uthman's Quran.

4 An interpretive text. This is the canonical text that may undergo reformulation for stylistic, practical, or dogmatic reasons.

A complicating factor is the role of oral communication in stage 1. The author could give more than one or several oral performances, and be recorded or remembered in different ways, and this would mean several versions vying for the status of being the original. There might be more than one original.

Potential for Quranic Textual Criticism

To fully achieve its purpose, textual criticism requires the comparison of a good number of relevant manuscripts, and as indicated above there is a lack of ancient Quran manuscripts. Those in power did what they could to destroy any variant copies of the Quran. However, some progress has been made with the discovery of a store of ancient manuscripts in Sanaa, in the Yemen. This is the subject of the next chapter.

~~~~

Chapter 15 – Sanaa 1

The Discovery

In 1965, heavy rain damaged the roof of the Western Library in the Great Mosque of Sanaa and during assessment of the damage a long-forgotten storeroom, without a door and with only a single window, was discovered. It contained a large collection of ancient Quranic manuscripts. Some were removed but the greater number bundled in sacks were only removed in 1972 when further building work was necessary. In the following years, the Yemeni authorities and various international experts discussed and examined how the manuscripts might be restored and preserved. [1]

In 1980, the Yemeni Department for Antiquities with funding of over 1 million Euros from the Cultural Section of the German Foreign Ministry was able to launch a project to restore and preserve these manuscripts. The local director was initially Gerd-Rudiger Puin of the University of Saarland and the project continued some eight years until 1989. As well as restoration, the work involved the design of permanent storage and the collation of parchment fragments to identify distinct Quranic manuscripts. [2]

There are altogether around 12,000 fragments most of which could be assigned to over 900 Qurans but none are complete and many consist of only a few folios. They are now located in the House of Manuscripts, the Dar al-Makhtutat (DAM), in Sanaa. [3]

One item in particular in this huge find has attracted great attention following the announcement of its existence in 1985. It is a very rare Quranic palimpsest. A palimpsest is a manuscript where the original text has been erased and new text written in its place. Over time the original text begins to reappear and some of it can still be read. This obviously has the potential for revealing something about the history of the Quran. The Sanaa palimpsest has the catalogue number DAM 01-27.1

The Palimpsest – Sanaa 1

There is some uncertainty, and potential confusion, concerning the number of folios that correctly belong to the palimpsest identified by DAM 01-27.1. In the House of Manuscripts itself, 38 folios have been assigned to that catalogue entry.

There are a further four folios in private hands. It appears that before the manuscripts discovered in the Grand Mosque were safely secured four folios from the palimpsest were removed and found their way to auction houses and between 1992 and 2008 auctioned in London. They are now referred to as Christies 2008, Stanford 2007, David 86/2003, and Bonhams 2000.

Scholars Elisabeth Puin, Behnam Sadeghi and Mohsen Goudarzi, also believe two folios in DAM 01-27.1 are incorrectly classified and belong to another catalogue entry DAM 01-25.1. And, according to Eleonore Cellard, a third folio may also be misplaced. [4]

It was also realised in 2012 that at least 37 folios conserved in the Eastern Library of the Grand Mosque in Sanaa and reproduced in edited form in a 2004 publication, could be detached folios of the upper text of DAM 01-27.1. [5]

The folios were the subject of researcher Razan Ghassan Hamdoun's master's thesis *The Quranic Manuscripts In Sanaa From The First Century Hijra And The Preservation Of The Quran* submitted to Yemenia University in 2004. The folios studied by Hamdoun include palimpsests that might belong to DAM 01-27.1, despite some differences in size. Further research is needed. [6]

To help avoid confusion over what is being discussed scholars Sadeghi and Goudarzi introduced a label for the complete manuscript that includes the folios that are correctly assigned to DAM 01-27.1, the four auctioned folios, and any that might surface in the future. They call the whole manuscript Sanaa 1.

Work So Far

The following sections introduce and summarise recent major studies of Sanaa 1 especially the lower layer. Mentioned here in this first section is important earlier work.

Alba Fedeli

Alba Fedeli in 2005 was the first to publish a study of the lower text. [7] She examined two of the auctioned folios, Bonhams 2000 and David 86/2003 and pointed out several variants with the Uthman text. She noted three of them are mentioned in the literature as Companion codices' variants.

Photographic Work

Gerd Puin, the first local director of the restoration project, did not share the microfilms of the DAM 01-27.1 folios that he possessed and interested scholars would have had to travel to Sanaa to see the microfilms available there. [8]

Matters were greatly improved in 2007 when Sergio Noja Noseda took high-resolution photographs including ultraviolet images of the DAM 01-27.1 folios as part of a project founded by Christian Robin. [9]

Elisabeth Puin

Starting in 2008 Elisabeth Puin, wife of Gerd Puin, made use of her husband's images, small 6x6" photographs in black and white, and published a series of four papers which included the transcription of the lower text of several folios. [10]

SADEGHI, BERGMANN, AND GOUDARZI

The following sections give a summary of the findings of two major studies and the research involved.

Behnam Sadeghi and Uwe Bergmann, *The codex of the companion of the Prophet and the Quran of the Prophet,* (2010). The authors examine the four auctioned Sanaa 1 folios and nine leaves from DAM 01-27.1 for which they had images. [11]

Behnam Sadeghi and Mohsen Goudarzi, *Sanaa 1 and the Origins of the Quran,* (2012). This study covers and examines all the folios believed to correctly belong to the palimpsest of DAM 01-27.1 and the four auctioned folios, 40 folios in total. [12]

The 35 folios in which amounts of the lower text can be read cover some 1700 verses representing about 27% of the Quran, and of these about 860 verses can be read, about 14% of the Quran. [13]

The significance of this work is clearly stated:

The lower text of Sanaa 1 is at present the most important document for the history of the Quran. As the only known extant copy from a textual tradition beside the standard Uthmanic one, it has the greatest potential of any known manuscript to shed light on the early history of the scripture. [14]

Date of Lower Writing

Based on the writing style and art-historical considerations the lower writing almost certainly comes from the seventh century CE, and probably the earlier part of that century. Combined with the fact that the lower text contains Sura 9 which includes some of the last revelations from the Prophet this implies the text was written not long after the Prophet died in 632 CE.

Based on radiocarbon dating carried out by the Accelerator Mass Spectrometry (AMS) Laboratory at the University of Arizona, the Sanaa 1 parchment has a 95% probability of coming from the period 578–669 CE and a 68% probability of coming from the period 614–656 CE. [15]

The date of the parchment is a good indicator of the date of the writing as it is very likely that any parchment was used for writing very soon after it was created. Such a valuable and scarce material would not lie unused for long and so the lower writing is about as old as the parchment on which it appears.

Another useful way of viewing the radiocarbon results shows the probabilities of the parchment being older than certain dates.

Table 4 – Probability of Sanaa 1 Being Older than Specific Years as Shown by Radiocarbon Dating

Older than Year CE	% Probability
671	99
661	95.5
646	75.1

Another factor supporting the creation of Sanaa 1 in the first half of the seventh century is that after Uthman's standardisation around 650 CE, copying non-standard Qurans became less common, and only a few held on to their Companion versions.

The Research

Text Types – C-1 a Different Text Type

The outstanding feature of the Sanaa 1 lower text is that it does not belong to the Uthman textual tradition to which almost all extant Quranic manuscripts belong. It is a different text type which is designated C-1. [16]

It is also different from the text types represented by the Companion codices of Ibn Mas'ud and Ubayy b. Ka'b based on what is known about them from early literary sources.

Uthman texts may have many differences among themselves and exhibit a range of variants but these differences are minor when compared with the variants found in other text types such as C-1 or Ibn Mas'ud text which have their own range of variants even if some are similar.

Some C-1 variants are the same as those reported in the codices of Ibn Mas'ud and Ubayy b. Ka'b but they are a minority of C-1 variants. C-1 does not share the vast majority of its variants with these codices, nor are the majority of their variants found in C-1. C-1 is a distinct "Companion codex" text type. Examples of variants are given below. A text type is thus a cluster of similar texts which stand apart from other clusters.

The analysis and comparison of the text types of a particular work can produce a family tree which throws light on the original work, in this case, the prototype disseminated by the Prophet Muhammad, and how it was transmitted.

The Family Tree

Textual criticism is used to determine the relationship between the Uthman, Ibn Mas'ud and C-1 text types; is one text type older than the other, possibly being its source, is one more accurate, and how do they relate to a common prototype? Allied to this is a determination of the right model for textual transmission.

One form of analysis, known as stemmatics, examines the frequency with which each text agrees with each of the others and produces a family tree showing how the text types are related. A second approach, polarity analysis, examines the nature of the differences and shows which text type is likely to be earlier. [17]

The differences in the Uthman text type are mostly those associated with the copying of manuscripts or the correction of dictation against a manuscript whereas the relatively larger differences with C-1 are more to do with orality. The analysis also suggests that Uthman's text type wording is older than that of C-1.

There are a number of possible family trees but two are the most promising. [18]

Diagram 2 – Most Promising Family Trees

Key: P=Prototype, U=Uthman version, IM=Ibn Mas'ud version.

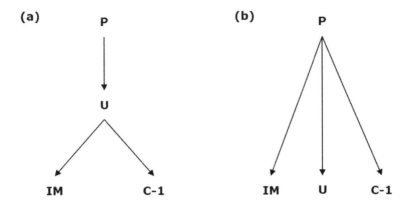

Of these two the most plausible is (b)

The above analysis assumes that Uthman's codex is an independent work. There is another possibility. Uthman's codex could be a hybrid work based on a number of Companion codices, perhaps the result of an effort to find consensus. This would give the following family tree.

Diagram 3 – Family Tree for Uthman's Codex as a Hybrid Work

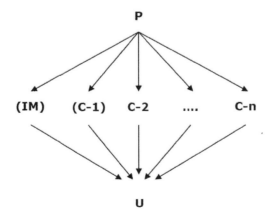

The Findings

The Authenticity of Companion Codices

The existence and characteristics of C-1 confirm much of what the early literary sources say about no longer extant Companion codices. C-1 both shares some of the variants and exhibits the same kind as the early sources report for Companion codices. There is every reason to believe codices such as Ibn Mas'ud's existed and the information about them is well preserved. [19]

When they were created is also confirmed. The textual criticism producing the family tree above shows the beginnings of the C-1 text type go back before the distribution of the standard Uthman text type circa 650 CE. Companion codices really go back to the time of the Companions.

How Transmission Took Place

The major differences between the C-1 and Uthman text types suggest a process in which the prototype was recited in a dictation like manner, though not word-by-word, and was taken down by scribes in somewhat different ways. A text so produced was copied and copied again, and even again, creating a textual tradition and a family of closely related texts such as the C-1 text type. [20]

Composition of the Suras

The analysis of C-1 and its comparison with other textual traditions answers one of the most important questions about the early history of the Quran; who put the verses together to form the suras?

The mainstream traditional view and that of some modern scholars, such as Arthur Jeffery, is that the suras were composed after the Prophet's death. The task is given to the committee appointed by Uthman during his rule circa 650 CE, to collect and standardise the Quran.

C-1 shows the suras were composed earlier and supports the less common view that the sequences of verses and sentences were fixed in the Prophetic prototype. The Uthman, C-1, and Companion text types generally have the same passages within suras, they show great agreement, and this must mean the suras were fixed that way before the various text types split from one another to form the family tree. [21]

The order of suras, however, was not fixed, and C-1 and the other types show significant sura order differences.

The point can also be made that the traditions in the early literature that mention the different sura orders in the Companion codices would make no sense if the suras had not been formed.

The findings also question the traditions about the last-minute discovery of the last two verses of Sura 9 that were found only with one man named Khuzayma, or Abu Khuzayma, or Ibn Khuzayma. C-1 has these verses and there are no reports that they are missing in any other Companion codex. The verses must have belonged to the prototype.

Reliability of Uthman's Version

The analysis that produces the (a) and (b) family trees also suggests Uthman's text gives the most accurate reproduction of the prototype. [22] Where there is disagreement in the C-1, Uthman, and Ibn Mas'ud texts, the Uthman text usually agrees with one against the other.

The family tree shown in Diagram 3 where the Uthman text has been created by comparing other codices and the selection of the most common reading where there is disagreement also explains this observation.

Based on only nine folios, this finding is provisional. The folios available after the analysis indicate the picture is more complicated and it is not yet clear if one text is the most reliable.

Scale and Examples of Variants

The greatest number of variants exhibited by C-1 in comparison with the Uthman text are additions, omissions, transpositions, and substitutions of entire words and sub-word elements (morphemes). They involve elements of language such as suffixes, prefixes, prepositions, and pronouns or involve changes of person, tense, mood, or voice (passive or active), or the use of different words having the same root.

The folios subject to this detailed examination, that is, the four auctioned Sanaa 1 folios in which nearly all the lower text is readable, cover some 90 verses of the Quran. The research found the following number of major variants in the C-1 text compared with the Uthman text.

Additions   9
Omissions   14
Substitutions   8
Total   31

Thus, one in three verses displays a major variant. [23] Table 5 gives some examples. [24]

Table 5 - Examples of Major Variants

Quranic verse	The text of the standard Uthman tradition	The text of the C-1 tradition
2.196	Do not shave your heads until the offering reaches its destination	Do not shave until the offering reaches its destination
2.196	If any of you be sick	Should one of you be sick
2.196	fasting, or alms, or an offering	fasting or an offering
2.201	There are people who say, "Our Lord, give us in this world", and they have no portion in the world to come. Then, there are those	There are people who say, "Our Lord, give us in this world", and they have no portion in the world to come. Then, there are those

	who say, "Our Lord, give us good in this world and good in the next".	who say, "Our Lord, give us in this world and the next".
63.7	They are the ones who say, "Do not spend (alms) on those who are with the Messenger of God in order that they may disperse".	They are the ones who say, "Do not spend (alms) on those who are with the Messenger of God in order that they may disperse from around him".

Very exceptionally variants are at the level of sentences or verses. For example, C-1 has the two short, three word, verses 31 and 32 in Sura 20 in reverse order, and a short verse of Sura 9 is missing.

Q 9:85 *Do not let their possessions and their children impress you: God means to punish them through these in this world, and that their souls should depart while they disbelieve.*

OTHER RESEARCH AND FINDINGS

Another major study is published in Asma Hilali's book, *The Sanaa Palimpsest: The Transmission of the Quran in the First Centuries AH* (2017). She provides a new annotated edition of the two layers of the Sanaa palimpsest together with a critical introduction. [25]

Hilali has a different approach to that taken in previous work on Sanaa 1 which concentrated on dating and variants and identifying the textual traditions to which the upper and lower layers belong. Previous research assumed the folios were what was left of two complete Qurans. She focuses on *"philological analysis of the manuscript and the dynamic link between the successive layers of writing, correcting, decorating, erasing, rewriting, etc"*. She is primarily concerned with the stages and context of manuscript production and copying and raises fundamental questions about the written transmission of the Quran in the early centuries of Islam. [26]

Hilali argues that both the lower text and the upper text probably represent collections of disparate leaves that are not part of a particular Quran codex or at least do not refer to a Quran codex in its final shape. *"Both layers represent unfinished works of writing down Quran passages"*.

This is supported by evidence of multiple stages of correction, and, for the lower text, reading instructions. It indicates there are two incomplete and fragmented Quranic texts.

The Lower Text

Hilali determines that the lower text was written in a fragmentary way. The writer was putting passages together for his personal use. He was producing a type of aide-memoire possibly in the context of a Quran teaching circle, that would call for educational elements in writing and reading. In support of this Hilali notes the writer *"intentionally preserved copy errors or instructions"*. There is what must be the oldest example of a reading instruction in the text.

There are gaps in both the material and text of the leaves of DAM 01-27.1 and it does not make a coherent whole. Other factors include fluctuations in the form of letters, the density of writing and how verses and suras are separated, which indicate a single non-professional copyist, copying his text under dictation.

Regarding the work of Sadeghi and Goudarzi, Hilali states her study *"does not refute"* the hypothesis that the lower text is derived from an early Companion codex related to Ibn Mas'ud's codex. However, her assessment of the lower text questions the reconstruction that enabled the hypothesis.

The Upper Text

Hilali's analysis of the upper text shows that it has a mix of handwriting, four successive copyists, and mixes of verse markings, and in the way suras are separated, only some having artistic illuminations. It suggests a fragmentary and unfinished work the creation of which has been interrupted. The mixes also suggest the scribes and decorators did not have a common Quranic source. It appears there was no unified organisation for producing the manuscript and it is not part of a single codex.

Hilali goes on to say *"I would suggest that even if the Sanaa palimpsest is confirmed to be part of an original whole, the characteristics of the script in its leaves show that the text was composed in several discordant steps with large chronological gaps".*

"There is a crucial need for a codicological study of the manuscript kept in Sanaa and of the additional folios in order to confirm whether they are part of the same codex".

Counter Arguments

Hilali's take on the fragmentary and incomplete nature of the Sanaa texts has been challenged. Regarding the lower text, Nicolai Sinai [27] notes that Hilali examined some 10 folios compared with some 35 by Sadeghi and Goudarzi and had less success in reading what the lower text said.

He thinks the fact that both layers lack uniformity in various ways is not exceptional for a Quranic codex produced at such an early time. For example, such variation is found in the Codex Parisino-Petropolitanus and the Codex Amrensis. And, a reading instruction is not incompatible with the lower layer having once been a complete Quran.

Sinai says the strongest argument that the folios of DAM 01-27.1 originally belonged to a complete Quranic codex *"is their unfailingly sequential arrangement of verses on those folios or parts thereof that can still be deciphered".* And the lower layer, whether or not it was completed, contained a run of suras arranged in a way that was commonly found in Quranic codices. Such a sequence of verses and suras is not what one would expect of a collection of scribal exercises.

Dates of the Sanaa 1 Texts

Sadeghi and Bergmann conclude the lower text must have been written very soon after the death of Muhammad in 632 CE and before Uthman's standardisation efforts circa 650 CE. The radiocarbon results play a big part in this dating.

As noted above radiocarbon dating can give misleading results and it is desirable to check its findings against other dating methods. [Chapter 17 explains how radiocarbon dating works.]

François Déroche, in his book *Qurans of the Umayyads: A First Overview* (2013), says the orthography of the upper text suggests it was written in the eighth century.

Regarding the lower text, he notes there are a few examples of the use of improved Arabic writing, and though this is not a conclusive sign of a later date, it suggests the lower text was written when such improvements in Quranic orthography were underway.

Also, the use of *"sura titles and of decorative devices between the suras point to a later date in the first/seventh century"*. Such devices were not found in early copies like the Codex Parisino-Petropolitanus but were added later. Based on these points, Déroche suggests the lower text *"was written during the second half of the first/seventh century and erased at the earliest by the middle of the following century"*. [28]

~~~~

Chapter 16 – The Birmingham Quran

What Happened

The manuscript known as the Birmingham Quran consists of two folios which contain verses 17-31 of Sura 18, verses 91-98 of Sura 19, and verses 1-40 of Sura 20.

The folios are part of a collection of over 3000 ancient Middle Eastern manuscripts, known as the Mingana Collection, brought together by Alphonse Mingana, a famous Western scholar, in the late 1920s. His work was funded by Edward Cadbury of the chocolate business based in Birmingham and he made several trips to the Middle East. The collection eventually passed to the Cadbury Research Library at Birmingham University in the late 1990s. [1]

The two folios were originally stored with seven others and given the catalogue number M. 1572, and experts, at least from as early as 2009, were well aware that all nine manuscripts were very early and possibly from the 7th century CE.

Dr. Alba Fedeli, in 2011 during an in-depth palaeographic study of the folios for her PhD research, proposed that two of the folios belonged to a different manuscript than the other seven and could be older. The two (now M. 1572a) were most likely from the same codex manuscript as BnF Arabe 328c, part of a collection of folios in the Bibliotheque Nationale of Paris, and the other seven (now M. 1572b) part of codex Marcel 17, in the National Library of Russia, St Petersberg and Ms. 67 in the Museum of Islamic Art, Doha, Qatar. [2]

The great antiquity of the Birmingham Quran folios was well understood and they could be viewed online from as early as 2009 but in 2015 they shot to fame thanks to the BBC.

Following interest in the folios from those involved in the Corpus Coranicum project [See Chapter 14] the Cadbury Research Library had the folios radiocarbon dated by Oxford University's Radiocarbon Accelerator Unit in 2014. They came back with the result that there was a 95% probability the date of production of the folios' parchment was in the range 568-645 CE. This result was made public through the BBC in an article entitled "'*Oldest' Koran Fragment's found in Birmingham University*". [3]

The fact that they could be the "oldest" was very exciting, but if the folios were written sometime between 568 and 645 CE it raised some very interesting questions. Just over half this time span, 42 of 77 years, is before the date the Prophet began to receive revelations in 610 CE.

Reactions

Traditionist and revisionist scholars each concentrated on the end of the date range that supported their views; i.e., before Muhammad's revelations, or during his prophethood while he was teaching them. [4]

Good News

David Thomas, Professor of Christianity and Islam at Birmingham University, observed that the scribe who wrote the manuscript "*might have heard the Prophet Muhammad preach*", and the text of the manuscript demonstrated the Quran had "*undergone little or no alteration*".

Pre-Islamic Literature

The parts of Suras 18 and 20 covered by the Birmingham folios tell the story of Moses, have content concerning Dhul Qarnayn, usually assumed to be Alexander the Great, and tell the Christian story of the Seven Sleepers of Ephesus. The Sura 19 verses are a retelling of the Virgin Birth of Jesus Christ. [5]

It was quickly pointed out that all this content closely resembled and could be derived from pre-existing Christian literature. The folios were not part of the Quran but material later incorporated in the Quran, showing Muhammad used existing material and shaped it to fit the Islamic agenda.

Whatever the background of the verses in the Birmingham folios, the 16 folios of BNF BnF Arabe 328c which is part of the codex to which the Birmingham folios are believed to belong, cover some 400 verses of typical Quranic text.

Undermines Uthman Traditions

Scholars also quickly noted the date range for the parchment is almost all before Uthman's rule (r. 644–656 CE). The text is close to the Uthman standard and it does not appear to be a scrap or Companion variant missed by Uthman's campaign to destroy variant copies. Thus, if the date range is correct it undermines the traditions concerning Uthman's collection of the Quran, which is usually taken as circa 650 CE, well into his rule, and the time the Quran was put into its final written form. [6]

Media Distortion

Wider media coverage jumped on two words in the BBC headline, "oldest" and "found". Despite the BBC's use of single quotes for 'oldest' in its headline, the popular media took it to be the one and only, it was the oldest! It was the most famous! This was in striking contrast to the way scholars had the good sense to describe it; namely as "among the earliest in existence"; "one of the oldest fragments of the Koran in the world"; "so old"; "one of the oldest fragments of the Koran in the whole world"; "among the very oldest surviving texts of the Koran". It is simply wrong to claim that any extant Quranic manuscript holds the record as the oldest. [7]

"Found" too gave great scope for journalistic twists to the story. The finder had to find it by chance, it was hidden away, and nobody was looking for anything new. An extreme example of this was given by the Huffington Post.

A Ph.D. student who stumbled upon several ancient pieces of paper hidden in another book may have inadvertently discovered pages from the world's oldest Quran, researchers at the University of Birmingham in England announced Wednesday.

The 1948–63 catalogue had given the date of the folios as from the 8th to 9th century CE according to much earlier studies, but as noted above, scholars were well aware, at least since 2009, that the folios might date from the 7th century CE.

Dating Issues

Another aspect of public reaction was the confidence in and consequent appeal of a scientific dating method such as radiocarbon dating. Such dating contrasts with the caution scholars often express with dating based on expert and judgemental methods such as palaeography.

However, there are questions about radiocarbon dating and these are examined in the next chapter and are only touched on here.

Radiocarbon dating gives the date of the creation of the parchment not the writing on it, though most scholars believe writing took place very soon after a parchment was produced because it was very expensive and would not be left unused for decades or even years.

It was important to determine if the Birmingham folios were not a palimpsest, in which the original writing had been erased, and as in the Sanaa example, the parchment used for a later text. In 2017 Birmingham University commissioned a project involving multi-spectral imaging which examines the manuscript through different wavelengths of light. The results showed no hidden text proving that it is not a palimpsest and the visible writing is the first use of the parchment as a manuscript. [8]

Other research commissioned by Birmingham has identified the types of inks used on the manuscript and shown that the brown ink is a kind used since the 5th century and the red ink a kind used since before the current era but as yet there is no scientifically reliable method for determining the age of ink.

Palaeography

Scholars have noted various aspects of the writing and layout of the text strongly suggest a manuscript from a later time than the dates given by radiocarbon dating. It has a well-established page layout, a developed Hijazi script style, some dashes to distinguish consonants, verse numbering, and sura divisions, which are not associated with the very earliest manuscripts.

Yasin Dutton [9] notes the writing is highly unlikely to predate Uthman's standardisation which took place around 650 CE. The text is overwhelmingly Uthmanic. One would expect more variants—and more extensive variation—in any *mushaf* written before that time such as is recorded for various Companion codices.

Mustafa Shah, from the Islamic studies department of the School of Oriental and African Studies in London, says *"When we look at the style of the manuscript, at the date, the use of diacritics, the style of the consonants, the verse markers, all of these fix it to the Umayyad period"*. The Umayyad dynasty ruled the Islamic caliphate from 661 CE until 750 CE. *"The fact that it belongs to the Umayyad period should not diminish its historical importance. It corroborates the traditional accounts of the way in which the Quran was brought together"*. He also noted most scholars would not rely only on radiocarbon dating for dating an early manuscript. [10]

Early dating of the Birmingham Quran has also been queried on palaeography grounds by scholars in the Middle East. Saud al-Sarhan, Director of Research at the King Faisal Centre for Research and Islamic Studies in Riyadh mentions the use of dots and separated chapters. He is supported by other Saudi-based experts who say the Birmingham Quran could not have been written during the Prophet's lifetime because its sura decoration, marked verse endings, and coloured inks, were not in use then, and Qurans did not follow any standard sequence of suras. [11]

Future Research

Stepping back from the issues and the excitement caused by misleading press coverage Alba Fedeli has proposed a scholarly way forward. [12] The Birmingham Quran is part of a larger group of early Quranic manuscripts, and by itself, its two leaves can only provide limited information about the state of the text at the beginning of Islam.

We need to *"explore all of the early Quranic manuscripts to detect those signs that can tell the story of their production. Scholars know very little about these fragments, their place of production, time, travels, use and reuse, corrections. Two numbers, i.e. 568–645, don't tell us a lot"*.

Phylogenetic software for creating family trees that show how different items are related applied to the manuscripts of which the Birmingham Quran is one small item will help us understand the connections between manuscripts, the first part of the story.

~~~~

Chapter 17 – Radiocarbon Dating

How it Works

The parchment on which ancient manuscripts are written is made from the hides of animals, mainly sheep, calves, and goats. Like all living things these animals while they are alive absorb carbon from the Earth's atmosphere. This includes carbon 14 (C-14), an isotope of carbon that slowly breaks down at a regular rate to carbon 12 (C-12), the stable form of carbon. [1]

Once an animal dies it stops absorbing carbon but the breakdown of C-14 to C-12 continues, and the ratio of C-14 to C-12 in the remains of an animal gives a measure of how long it is since the animal stopped absorbing carbon, in other words, when it died.

Over the millennia the level of C-14 in the atmosphere changes and years given by C-14/C-12 ratio measurements are not the same as calendar years. A calibration curve is needed to convert C-14 years to calendar years. The current version of the curve is INTCAL13 based on historical data from North America and Europe. It is assumed that the diffusion of C-14 is fast enough to nullify any local or seasonal effects.

The date of a parchment sample as indicated by the date the animal died that provided the parchment hide is not necessarily the date the parchment was used for writing but most scholars take the view parchment was not stored for decades or even years before being written on. Parchment was an expensive and highly prized material. Its production might require the large part of a herd of animals to fulfil a commission for a written work.

The Problem

The scientific basis of radiocarbon dating gives the method great appeal and its use is increasing but it is not one hundred per cent reliable. It is known to give results that are wrong and dates that are too early as judged by the weight of palaeographic (writing) and philological (language) evidence, and other historical considerations.

In his book the *Qurans of the Umayyads: A First Overview*, François Déroche gives some examples. He discusses the famous "Quran of the Nurse" that has both a colophon and deed of *waqf* (donation) that date it to 1020 CE. Using radiocarbon dating a French laboratory gave the result that the date of this Quran was in the range 871–986 CE with a probability of 95%, and there was a 99% probability that the date was 937 CE or earlier. [2]

The top end of the date range is 34 years too early, and the most probable date, 937 CE, 83 years too early.

Déroche also refers to further radiocarbon dating of Sanaa 1 folios organised by Christian Robin, a French scholar of early Arabic. A laboratory in Lyon dated several fragments and dated one to 543–643 CE and another to 433–599 CE with 95% probabilities. There was a third that gave the extremely early date range of 388–535 CE and the possibility of sample contamination or faulty chemical pre-treatment has to be considered.

Table 6 – Radiocarbon Dating of Sanaa 1 Palimpsest

Laboratory	95% Probability in the Date Range CE:
Arizona for Sadeghi and Bergmann in 2010 (on Stanford 07 folio)	578 – 669
Lyons (on other folios)	543 – 643 433 – 599
Oxford	Similar to Arizona
Kiel	430 – 610

One of the folios was sent to be tested at two other laboratories, one in Oxford and one in Kiel. Table 6 compares these results including the original Sanaa 1 dating published by Sadeghi and Bergmann in 2010. [See above in Chapter 15] [3]

Déroche suggests that regional climatic factors may have a part in giving radiocarbon dating a tendency to give earlier dates than other dating methods. He thinks the most sensible approach is to use all relevant methods such as palaeography, art historical features, and orthography when determining a date range for a manuscript. Radiocarbon dating is best at providing a first indication but it needs to be improved before it can be relied on for accurate dating to within periods of less than a century.

Recent Research

Déroche's suggestion that regional climate may cause radiocarbon dating inaccuracies is given strong support by research published in 2018. [4] Archaeologist Sturt Manning and colleagues from Cornell University show variations in the radiocarbon cycle at certain periods of time affect standards used in archaeological and historical research in the area covered by Israel, southern Jordan and Egypt.

The standard INTCAL13 curve used to adjust radiocarbon dates for different amounts of atmospheric carbon at different times (see above) is based on measurements of radiocarbon levels in trees from Central and Northern Europe and North America and assumes at any given time radiocarbon levels are similar and stable everywhere across each hemisphere.

Manning's team have discovered trees growing in southern Jordan show a different amount of radiocarbon compared with trees in Central and Northern Europe and in North America. This may be a consequence of climatic changes, periods of warming and cooling modulating the local growing seasons.

Scholars working on Biblical chronology in Jordan and Israel are using a calibration curve that is not accurate for that region. Manning says his team's results *"should prompt a round of revisions and rethinking for the timeline of the archaeology and early history of the southern Levant through the early Biblical period"*.

Documenta Coranica, a project based at the Berlin-Brandenburg Academy of Sciences and Humanities and related to the Corpus Coranicum project [See Chapter 14], as part of its work conducted large-scale radiocarbon tests on samples from different Quran manuscripts, focusing on pieces believed to be from the 1st or 2nd century AH.

Dr. Eva Mira Youssef-Grob, one of the leaders of the project, has written a comprehensive account of the challenges, complexities, and best practices of radiocarbon dating. [5] She discusses the care needed in the use of calibration curves (such as INTCAL13) and, even when the most precise equipment is being used it is essential not rely on measurement from one sample, but to get results from at least two samples. Also, as more results become available from more manuscripts the comparison and modelling of results will help. Youssef-Grob concludes *"Under good conditions and with a careful experimental setup (with multiple samples, a favourable calibration curve, and using modelling), we might reach a highly probable 50-year window for dating, but day-to-day business is rather the assignment of a century"*.

~~~~

Chapter 18 – Other Manuscript Research

This chapter introduces recent examples of scholarly works on early Quranic manuscripts that are in part accessible to the layman and novice student. It would certainly help to be familiar with ancient Arabic writing to get the full benefits of these works but it is not essential to learn a lot from them. The first is Keith E. Small's book *Textual Criticism and Quran Manuscripts* published in 2011. [1]

Textual Criticism and Quran Manuscripts

Background and Objectives

Small points out that, as a rule, manuscripts of the Quran have not been subjected to the methods of textual criticism developed to determine the early history and origins of other sacred books or bodies of literature or to document their early transmission. Big problems are the lack of access to relevant manuscripts and the paucity of manuscripts, but both the Corpus Coranicum project [See Chapter 14, Extant Early Manuscripts] and the palimpsest manuscript discoveries in Yemen are very significant steps in remedying them.

There is also a great need to explore *"what can be achieved through a careful collation of textual variants from extant manuscripts and early Islamic literature"* and this is what Small sets out to do. Can existing early manuscripts be used to demonstrate what we might learn about the textual origins and history of the Quran?

The manuscript texts Small works on do not include any of the Yemen palimpsests but he says there are significant observations that can be made on all variants and it is hoped the methods used in his study will prove useful for any analysis of the palimpsest variants.

A Framework for Textual Criticism

The purpose of the textual criticism of ancient texts is usually defined as (a) the recovery or authentication of the original text, and (b) the tracing of its historical development. This may seem simplistic or even self-evident but in ancient times well-before printing when all text was hand-copied, and writing systems evolving, matters were complicated especially when *"dealing with a literary tradition that operates with a mixture of oral and written literary conventions"*.

Modern and popular Muslim opinion tends to state the text of the Quran is perfectly preserved since the time of Muhammad. This contrasts with early and medieval Islamic scholarship that recognised the potential for textual variation and missing text and tended not to claim transmission was perfect. The study of early manuscripts confirms what early Islamic scholarship had to say.

Spoken words or written text becoming a widely or universally recognised book does not happen all at once and involves several stages. For the Quran Small defines the stages shown below. He modifies a scheme developed for New Testament studies and has added the Authoritative text-form stage.

1. Predecessor text-form: the oral or written sources the author used.

2. Autographic text-form: the form the author wrote as it left his desk.

3. Authoritative text-form: a form of text that acquired a degree of local geographic consensual authority.

4. Canonical text-form: a form of the text that acquired a degree of wide geographic consensual authority.

5. Interpretive text-form: any later intentional reformulation for stylistic, practical, or dogmatic reasons.

[This is the basis of the framework already mentioned above in Chapter 14, Extant Early Manuscripts.]

If the spoken word is involved in stage 2 there might be a number of hearings or performances that could all be deemed "original".

The Studied Manuscripts

Small examines the variants found in seven Quran verses, Q 14:35-41, across 22 manuscripts, 19 of which date from the first four Islamic centuries AH, and three from the last two centuries. Only six have estimated age ranges that fall in or cover the first century AH, and thus the great majority of manuscripts if not all are after Uthman's collection and standardisation efforts and also mainly after Abd al-Malik's time. The manuscripts and their estimated age ranges are listed in Table 7 below.

The seven verses describe how Abraham settled his son in Mecca.

Small identifies nearly 350 variants across the 22 manuscripts and discusses them under the following headings.

Orthographic variants (the spelling of words)
Copyist mistakes
Diacritical mark variants and variants affecting grammar
Rasm variants
Variant verse divisions
Physical corrections to manuscripts

Table 7 – Manuscripts Studied

Manuscript	Location	Date Estimates Quoted by Small	
		AH	**CE**
Istanbul	Istanbul	First century [1]	Early Eighth 700–750
Topkapi	Istanbul	[2]	Late Seventh. Early Eighth 650–750
01-20.x	Sanaa, Yemen	Early Second	Mid to Late

		100–140 [1]	Eighth 750–800
01-28.1	Sanaa, Yemen	Late First 50–100 [1]	Early Eighth 700–750
01-29.1	Sanaa, Yemen	[1]	
BL Or. 2165	British Library	30–85 or First-Second [1]	650–704 or Seventh-Eighth
The Samarkand kufic Codex	Tashkent, Uzbekistan	Early Second 100–150 [2]	Late Eighth 750–800
BNF Arabe 325a	Bibliothèque Nationale de Français / Paris	Second 100–200 [2]	Eighth 700–800
BNF Arabe 326a	BNF / Paris	Second, possibly First [2]	
BNF Arabe 328a	BNF / Paris	Early to Mid First 0–75 [1]	
BNF Arabe 330a	BNF / Paris	Late Second 150–200 [2]	
BNF Arabe 331	BNF / Paris	Early Second 100–150 [2]	
BNF Arabe 332	BNF / Paris	Early Second 100–150 [2]	Late Eighth 750–800
BNF Arabe 333c	BNF / Paris	Third 200–300 [3]	Tenth 900–1000
BNF Arabe 334c	BNF / Paris	Late Second 150–200 [3]	Early Ninth 800–850
BNF Arabe 340c	BNF / Paris	Late Second to Early Third	Early to Mid Ninth

		150–250 [3]	800–850
Meknes		Late Second to Early Third 150–250 [3]	Early to Mid Ninth 800–850
BNF Arabe 343	BNF / Paris	Third to Fourth 200–400 [4]	Tenth to Eleventh 900–1100
BNF Arabe 370a	BNF / Paris	Late Third 250–300 [4]	Late Tenth 950–1000
BL Or. 12884	British Library	Manuscript fly-leaf states 340 [4]	Manuscript fly-leaf states 951
Mushaf Sharif	Istanbul	1093 [11]	1682
Warsh		Modern Printed Version	

The figures in brackets [] give the century AH given for a manuscript in the catalogue of its location library.

Findings

The great majority of variants concern the formation and spelling of words that do not affect the general meaning of the text. About 6% concern copyist mistakes. Only 5% of variants such as those concerning grammar or word variants affect the meaning, but even then in very minor ways. There is no change to the ideas or message of the Quran though it shows the Quran contains the changes that might be expected in ancient hand-copied manuscripts.

Small says this indicates the canonical text *rasm* was established early, probably around the mid-seventh century CE, and only the palimpsests give any indication of the pre-canonical *rasm*. The uniformity of the *rasm* in early manuscripts suggests that the text was canonised by a centralised political authority.

The studied manuscripts show *"an impressively controlled transmission"* reflecting the success of the efforts ascribed to Uthman (mid-seventh century CE), al-Hajjaj (early eighth century CE) and Ibn Mujahid (tenth century CE), to standardise the text of the Quran and to suppress textual variants.

Explanations and Implications

Small argues that because of the editing projects of Uthman and al-Hajjaj and the extensive testimony in the secondary literature that a much broader range of variants was once found in the Quran, the uniformity of the studied manuscripts is not evidence of a precisely transmitted autographic text-form. Also, the palimpsests even though showing recognisable Quranic material, contain variants involving different words and phrases.

What has been preserved is a version of the Quran chosen from a number of other versions and the standardisation and editorial projects carried out under the Umayyad caliphs resulted in the *"destruction of most if not all of the earliest manuscripts, with the result that it is currently impossible to recover the original form of the text"*.

It is not possible to determine what the earliest Muslims would have considered an Autographic text-form or the Authoritative text-forms of the Prophet's Companions. What has been preserved and transmitted is a version of one particular text put together between twenty and one hundred years after Muhammad's death. It is not possible to determine what editing might have been done to produce this version.

Small proposes that there never was a single original Autographic version of the Quran from which all other readings or textual versions, with whatever variations, must derive. He makes the bold claim *"the history of the transmission of the text of the Quran is at least as much a testament to the destruction of Quran material as it is to its preservation"*, and *"is also testimony to the fact that there never was one original text of the Quran"*.

Small defines and explains what he sees as the main periods of the Quran's historical development, the first period covering why this came about.

Period One: Muhammad's Prophetic Career (610–632 CE)

There does not seem to have been one written text in use during Muhammad's lifetime even though Quranic material was produced and used with his authority. Companions made and used their own collections of material. There was also a very strong oral tradition but it was not strong enough to establish a single vocalisation of the written text or to prevent or limit variations in the written text.

In the years immediately following Muhammad's death the various collections came into use as authoritative bodies of Quranic material. *"In this sense, the Quran could be said to have multiple original texts, each with both distinct and overlapping content in relation to the others"*.

It is thus not possible to recover one original text of the Quran; only original texts of the Quran or some of the loose body of material gathered by Muhammad's Companions. For a single Quran, the earliest stage of text available for reconstruction is an early edited Canonical text-form from Period Three listed below.

Period Two: The Companions' Collections (10–30 AH) (632–653 CE)

The recovery of material from this period is extremely difficult or even impossible. It was suppressed and destroyed during later caliphal standardisation projects. At best one can evaluate what the material was like from the variants described in the early literature. The examination of the lower texts in qualifying palimpsests and others that might be found will also be helpful.

The lack of manuscripts with variant texts agreeing with what is reported in early literature seems to confirm the effectiveness of their suppression and destruction.

Period Three: Uthman and al-Hajjaj (30–86 AH) (653–705 CE)
The version of the Quran reported to have been produced under Uthman (r. 644–656 CE) would be the first Canonical text-form and that organised by al-Hajjaj under Abd al-Malik (r. 685–705 CE) to refine and improve the consonantal base of the initial edition, an Interpretive text-form which itself became a new Canonical text-form of the consonantal text. It is also possible that there was only one project that later Islamic tradition made into two attributing it to both al-Hajjaj and Uthman to give it greater authority.

Western scholarship has produced three major views on the date of this codified early recension:

Early Codification. This view accepts that Uthman played the major role and was largely successful.

Later Codification. In this view codification was a later and gradual process or one predominantly organised by al-Hajjaj under caliph Abd al-Malik. The Quran did not take its present shape under Uthman but still within the Umayyad caliphate. Small believes that if precedence is given to manuscript evidence over tradition this is currently the best-supported view.

Late Codification. This Revisionist view that final codification did not take place until late Abbasid times (circa 750+ CE) seems to be contradicted by the manuscript evidence that the consonantal text and content existed in generally stable form during Umayyad times.

All views agree that distinctly Quranic material was present in the seventh century. They disagree on what kind of a form this material was in by c. 700 CE/81 AH and how well defined this material was as a body of written scripture.

Period Four: Editing and Development of Orthography (86–324 AH) (705–936 CE)
Though the basic consonantal text of the Quran was fixed in the third Islamic century it allowed flexibility in its vocalisation giving rise to the seven authoritative readings specified by Ibn Mujahid

(245–324 AH) (859–936 CE). Three further readings were allowed and four others gained recognition.

Although the documented extant material record is unclear historical records claim other versions existed and were recited. Al-Nadim, in his work *The Fihrist*, an index of all the books in Arabic in 375 AH, mentions the existence of manuscript copies of Ibn Mas'ud's and Ubayy b. Ka'b's versions and one attributed to Ali. Ibn Mas'ud and Ubayy b. Ka'b versions are also mentioned in 215 AH (830 CE) by al-Kindi, a Christian official in the Abbasid court.

Manuscript evidence for this period shows a great amount of experimentation in developing a comprehensive orthography for the Quran's text such as the use of coloured dots to signify pronunciation.

Small makes the point that Quranic textual criticism, as practised by Islamic scholars in the past, has not sought to determine the original Autographic text-forms or even its earliest Authoritative text-forms, but to justify one form of the text against others and this has resulted in the loss of the earliest Authoritative forms of the text.

Further periods defined by Small are:

Period Five: Consolidation of the Ten Readings (324–1342 AH) (936–1924 CE)

Period Six: Primacy of the Hafs text (1924/1342–The Present)

Qurans of the Umayyads: A First Overview

Objective and Method

In *Qurans of the Umayyads: A First Overview*, published in 2013, François Déroche explains how the *mushaf* evolved during the rule of the Umayyad caliphs (661–750 CE), effectively the first hundred years of the Quran as a written document. [2] He is especially concerned with how a manuscript can be dated to Umayyad times and dated within that period.

Early manuscripts are incomplete and lack colophons identifying the scribe and the production date of the manuscript. Scholars have to use other date indicators such as palaeography, orthography, art history, codicology and philology.

Déroche takes numerous features into account including; margins or lack thereof, ruling, page orientation (vertical or horizontal), letter forms, the presence or absence of sura dividers and their features (including their inks, elements, and whether they were original to the manuscript or added at a later time), other illuminations, number of lines per page, verse dividers and multi-verse dividers, and the bismillah being marked as a verse.

Findings
Déroche determines many manuscripts can be dated to Umayyad times and within that period there are two distinct stages; an early stage before Abd al-Malik during which the handwritten transmission of the text was diverse, fluid, and of an idiosyncratic Hijazi style, and a later stage, from Abd al-Malik onwards, when the text became sophisticated and unified and employed a much greater amount of illumination.

During the early decades of Umayyad rule, there was no strict control over the production and transmission of the text but most probably during Abd al-Malik's rule (65–86 AH) (685–705 CE) a much greater interest in the text and state sponsorship came about for two reasons, to achieve greater uniformity, and to support the prestige of the dynasty. Al-Hajjaj's "*Masahif* project" (84–85 AH) (703–704 CE) also points to this.

Given these factors and the increasing centralisation of the Islamic state, Déroche suggests Qurans might have been produced in state-sponsored workshops, or there were at least official guidelines for producing Qurans.

The Codex Parisino-Petropolitanus
Déroche attaches particular importance to the large Codex Parisino-Petropolitanus (CPP), a Hijazi manuscript dispersed across four collections, devoting the first of the four chapters of his

book to a summary of his studies of this manuscript. He determines that five scribes worked on the manuscript and, given the type of errors they made, were copying it from another written text.

If what tradition says about al-Hajjaj's reforms is true, and in light of the highly idiosyncratic style of the five copyists, Déroche suggests it was written down in the period 671–695 CE and is a genuine early Umayyad Quran. The CPP text has variants showing the *rasm* was not fully fixed but in terms of content, it is consistent with the text now known as the Quran.

Déroche finds that peculiar verse divisions in the CPP manuscript suggest scribes added short verses to fix rhyme problems created by non-rhyming longer verses. That such editing happened has long been suspected by critical scholars and a Muslim tradition describes something similar during Muhammad's lifetime, Muhammad accepting the scribe's suggestion and adopting the revision as his own. [See Chapter 7, Early Writing and Compilation.]

Déroche points out the CPP manuscript clashes with the Muslim tradition that Uthman ordered a standard version of the Quran to prevent the spreading of different readings. The CPP script, produced after Uthman, would not have achieved that because it is far too defective with hardly any diacritical markings and the few it had applied in different ways by the different scribes and no short vowels or orthoepic marks. The reader had to decide was a verb active or passive, was a word a noun or a verb, how words should be said, from the context or from memory.

Yasin Dutton, another modern scholar, when reviewing this observation says one must assume Uthman was concerned about major differences in the text that might cause—indeed, had caused—argument. [3] [See also Chapter 5, Variants.]

Corrections in Early Quran Manuscripts: Twenty Examples

Background

Dan Brubaker has surveyed some 10,000 pages of early Quran manuscripts and in his book *Corrections in Early Quran Manuscripts: Twenty Examples,* published in 2019, [4] he provides an overview to illustrate the general nature of the many physical changes or corrections found in early Quran manuscripts. He has found the subject is of interest to non-academic readers and the book is also an introduction to the subject written to be accessible to non-specialists.

Brubaker gives 20 examples from 18 Quranic manuscripts from the 7th–9th century CE and provides his views concerning the reasons some corrections may have occurred. The examples cover a representative range of change types, erasures, insertions, replacements (overwritten text), and coverings (sometimes with overwritten text), some of which Brubaker believes are not reasonably attributed to mere scribal error.

The Significance of Corrections

Brubaker sets out what he sees as the significance of so many corrections in the Quran during the first several centuries of Islam. What does their existence mean?

Firstly, even though most surviving Quran manuscripts (except the lower layer of the Sanaa palimpsest) show the signs of a campaign of standardisation as reported implemented by caliph Uthman, *"it is also clear that there existed some differences of perception about the correct words of the Quran text at the times most of these manuscripts were produced"* which were later revisited when these perceptions changed or standardisation became more effective. Possibly, these different perceptions came from particular regions or Islamic cities.

Secondly, the degree of flexibility is not great. The corrections in the manuscripts do not usually concern large portions of Quran text. Such limited flexibility beyond the decades following

Muhammad's death and extending for several centuries after appears to correspond with and support what is observed in other Islamic recordings such as the non-standard Quranic inscriptions in the Dome of the Rock completed in 691/2 CE and Nicolai Sinai's "emergent canon model" that the Quranic text, though achieving a recognizable form by 660 CE, continued to be reworked and revised until c. 700. [See Chapter 11, Closure of the Quran.]

Thirdly, they suggest a movement towards conformity to a standard over time. It was a gradual process. Brubaker claims this because at times the corrections are partial; where one item of writing on a page was revised but another that later was not standard was passed over, the scribe presumably not seeing it as incorrect.

Evidence for a Written Uthmanic Archetype

In his paper *"The Grace of God" as evidence for a written Uthmanic archetype: the importance of shared orthographic idiosyncrasies* (2019), Marijn van Putten examines the spelling of a particular word in 14 early Quranic manuscripts. [5]

The word *ni'mat* (grace) can be spelled two different ways and it appears in 23 places in each of these manuscripts. In the modern Cairo Quran it is spelled 12 times one way and 11 times the other way distributed randomly throughout the text showing there is no particular reason for it being spelled in a particular way in a particular context.

Van Putten shows the word nearly always has one of the two spellings in exactly the same place in every one of the early manuscripts studied. He argues this consistency can only be explained if these manuscripts are derived from a single written archetype, and given the estimated dates of the manuscripts examined, such a Quran archetype existed in the first century AH.

This consistency in spelling also implies that Quran manuscripts from the earliest days were copied from a written exemplar. Dictation and transcription of an oral tradition did not play a part.

Considering the early dates of the manuscripts, van Putten concludes *"it seems highly unlikely that this written archetype was standardised much later than the time of Uthman's reign"* and goes on to say it is even unlikely the archetype of the Uthmanic text postdates the canonical date given to it in the traditions, that is, during Uthman's rule (r. 644–656 CE), and most likely c. 650 CE.

The diagram below illustrates the estimated date ranges of the 14 manuscripts studied.

Diagram 4 – Early Manuscripts Date Ranges

AH	0	50	100	150
CE	610 620 630 640 **650** 660 670 680 690 700 710 720 730 740 750 760 770 780 790 800			

1 During the eight century CE (Deroche)
2 Second half of first century AH
3 652-763 CE (Radiocarbon)
4 First half second century AH
5 606-652 CE (Radiocarbon)
6 700-850 CE
7 Second half first century/early second AH
8 Eight/ninth century CE
9 Not before 700 CE
10 Third quarter first century AH
11 Before 750 CE
12 Late first/early second century AH
13 649-675 CE (Radiocarbon)
14 Later seventh/early eight century CE

Van Putten references earlier research that points strongly to this conclusion. In 2004 Michael Cook [6] published his analysis of 36 differences said to be found in the codices Uthman sent to the main Islamic cities, Kufa, Basra, Damascus, and the one kept in

Medina. [See Chapter 4] Such variants could arise during the copying process when the codices were created in Medina before being dispatched to the cities. Cook's source for these variants was a work on early Qurans by al-Dani (371–444 AH) a renowned Quran reader and traditionist scholar.

Cook's analysis of the variations showed there were a number of possible family relationships—stemmata—between and among these codices suggesting there had been genuine copying from an archetype. [See Chapter 15, Sanaa 1, for more on family tree analysis.]

Cook not having extant manuscripts, only reports about them found in later literature, might pose some questions. However, there is good evidence this literature provides accurate information on early manuscripts that no longer exist. Yasin Dutton shows in papers published in 2001 and 2004 that examples of what the literature says about early variant readings are found in very early manuscripts, thus supporting Cook's use of a secondary source and his argument for an early archetype. [7]

~~~~

ANNEX 1 – Early Muslim Literature – Traditions (Hadiths)

What we presently know of early Islam and the collection and codification of the Quran depends almost entirely on Muslim traditions. Traditions are also known as hadiths.

Description

During the first century of Islam, Arab culture still depended almost entirely on human memory and oral transmission for the communication of information. Paper had not been introduced to the region, writing materials were rare and very expensive, and Arab script at an early stage of development. Oral culture was popular and well entrenched.

Writing had only a limited role. Some who taught traditions used the scarce materials and elementary script to make notes for themselves as a memory support but their teaching and communication was all verbal.

Consequently, the Muslim traditions that we have are reports passed word-of-mouth from one generation to the next before being written down in a collection or used in a written historical or other literary work, when writing became more practical and widely practised in the second century AH, more than a 100 years after the time of the Prophet.

There are two parts to a tradition: the *matn*, the words of the report itself, what was said, what happened, etc; and the *isnad*, who made the report, and the chain of transmitters who passed it on to the time it was written down.

In the written form of a tradition the *isnad* precedes the *matn*, as follows: *"It has been related to me by A on the authority of B on the authority of C on the authority of D that E said (or did) ...."*. E could be a Companion of the Prophet or the Prophet himself.

The size of reports varies enormously, some are very short, a sentence or two, to reports that are like short stories, a thousand words or so (about two typed pages). The average is around 90 words.

What They Cover

Muslim traditions cover a vast range of subjects. Al-Bukhari's famous collection covers 97 topics, that can be classified as follows: Religious Instruction and Knowledge (24%); Prayer (12%); Military Campaigns and *Jihad* (12%); Family Life and Law (7%); Pilgrimage and Festivals (6%); Others (39%).

Other collections vary widely in what they cover.

Narrators and Numbers of Traditions

There are tens of thousands of traditions recorded in collections, one of the largest collections having some 27,000 traditions. There are significantly fewer tradition originators, that is, persons who first narrated reports. Chapter 6 above explains how 34 traditions concerning the collection of the Quran found in 19 collections can all be traced back to one person, a so-called common link.

A survey of tradition collections found 960 or so Companions originated traditions, but some Companions originated many more than others. The great majority of the 960 being responsible for only one or two or a handful, whereas a small number of Companions each originated very large numbers. Aisha, the Prophet's favourite wife, is the source for 2210 traditions and a household servant, Anas b. Malik, for 2286.

The same tradition report (*matn*) found with different chains of transmission (*isnads*) from the same original narrator are all counted as separate traditions. For example, the Companion Abu Hurayra, who knew the Prophet for less than three years, is given as the source of a tradition 5374 times in a later compilation of collections. After allowing for duplication of the same report this scales down to around 1700 distinct and different reports, nearly two reports per day over the time Abu Hurayra was with the Prophet.

Authenticity

Early Muslim scholars developed a system for judging the authenticity of individual traditions. It depended very much on knowledge of the persons named in a tradition's *isnad*: did that person have a good memory, a good reputation, were they trustworthy. This in turn depended on knowledge passed word-of-mouth from generation to generation and raises questions of reliability. Other factors, such as the number of persons that reported a particular saying, deed, or opinion, were also taken into account. Based on this kind of information traditions are classified as *sahih* (sound) or *hasan* (fair) or *da'if* (weak).

As noted above early modern Western scholars believed traditions were largely fabricated. They were the result of those living 150 or more years after the Prophet, when the written tradition collections were created, projecting their ideas and beliefs back onto the Prophet and his time. For example, there are traditions with anachronisms; the Prophet talking about something that did not exist in his lifetime or happened only afterwards. There are traditions concerning the rivalry for the caliphate or suppressing dissent and protecting those in power, that obviously have a political motive.

More recent research by Western scholars shows that examples of traditional material dated from 150–200 years or more after the life of the Prophet can be traced to dates much closer to the Prophet's lifetime.

The Collections

There are several different kinds of collections. (These are mainly referred to as hadith collections, and the term 'hadith' will be used.)

Musannafs

The earliest surviving collections are *musannafs* organised by topic and including mainly reports of Companions, the opinions of Muslim scholars, and the views of the *musannaf* author himself. Prophetic hadiths, reports concerning what the Prophet said or did, are in the minority. They cover Islamic legal practice on matters such as ritual, prayer, and inheritance. One of the earliest surviving *musannafs* is the *Muwatta'* of Malik b. Anas (93–179 AH) which contains 1720 reports of which 527 are Prophetic hadiths. *Muwatta'* means "well-trodden, agreed path".

Musnads

Another early type of hadith collection is the *musnad*. These concentrate on Prophetic hadiths listed by the Companion or Companions originating the report.

The best known *musnad* was produced by Ahmad b. Hanbal (164–241 AH) and contains about 27,000 hadiths. This very high number includes repetitions, counting the same *matn* with different *isnads* as separate hadiths. Ignoring these *isnad* variations the number of distinct *matns* is estimated to be about 5200.

Ibn Hanbal himself said some of the hadiths were weak and another scholar estimated only 57% are *sahih* (sound), and 24% are *da'if* (weak). The weak hadiths include the tradition that some text in the early Quran was lost because it was eaten by a goat.

Sunans

Sunans are similar to *musannafs*, designed to be used as legal references and organised by topic, but they use only Prophetic hadiths with complete *isnads*. The authors of such collections also sought to use what they believed to be authentic hadiths, those with convincing *isnads*, or because they had wide support amongst scholars.

The increased interest in Prophetic hadiths and in knowing if they were genuine led to the six canonical collections. These are emphasized in the Table below.

Ignoring repetitions and allowing for overlap there are about 9500 different hadiths in the six canonical works. The two most famous are *Sahih* al-Bukhari, giving some 2500 reports after allowing for duplication, and *Sahih* Muslim and they are regarded as genuine Islamic sacred books by Sunni Muslims.

Tradition (Hadith) Collections (up to 500 AH)		
Collector	**Lifetime or Year Died AH**	**Titles or Types of Works**
Second Century AH		
Ibn Jurayj	150	*Musannaf*
Ma'mar b. Rashid	154	*Musannaf*
Abu Hanifa	156	*Musnads*. Compiled by students
Sufyan al-Thawri	161	*Musannaf*
Malik b. Anas	93–179	*Al-Muwatta'*, *Musannaf*
Abu Yusuf	182	*Musannaf*
al-Tayalisi [1]	133–204	*Musnad*
al-Shafi'i	150–204	*Musnad*. Compiled by students
Abd al-Razzaq [1]	126–211	*Musannaf*
Third Century AH		
al-Humaydi	219	*Musnad*
Sa'id b. Mansur al-Khurasani	227	*Sunan*
al-Musaddad	228	*Musnad*
Ibn Abi Shayba	156–235	*Musannaf*
Ishaq b. Rahawayh	238	*Musnad*
Ahmad b. Hanbal [1]	164–241	*Musnad*
Abu Muhammad Abd al-Hamid b. Humayd	249	*Musnad*
al-Darimi	181–255	*Sunan*
al-Bukhari [1]	**194–256**	*Sahih*
Muslim	**204–261**	*Sahih*

Ibn al-Najjar	262	*Musnad*
Ibn Majah	**209–273**	***Sunan***
Abu Dawud	**202–275**	***Sunan***
Baqi b. Makhlad	201–276	*Musnad*
al-Tirmidhi [1]	**209–279**	***Jami'***
al-Harith b. Abi Usama	282	*Musnad*
Abu Muslim al-Kashshi	282	*Sunan*
Abu Bakr al-Bazzar	292	*Musnad*
al-Nasa'i [1]	**224–303**	***Sunan***
Fourth Century AH		
Abu Ya'la al-Mawsili [1]	307	Musnad
al-Tabari [1]	224–310	*Musnad, Tahdhib al-Athar*
Ibn Khuzaymah	312	*Sahih*
Abu al-Qasim al-Baghawi	317	*Mu'jam al-Sahaba*
Abu Awana	317	*Musnad*
Ali b. Hamshadh al-Nishapuri	338	*Musnad*
Ibn Hibban	354	*Sahih*
al-Tabarani	360	*al-Mu'jam al-Kabeer*
al-Hasan al-Masarjisi al-Nishapuri	365	*Musnad*
Abu Bakr al-Isma'ili	371	*Mu'jam al-shuyukh*
al-Daraqutni	306–385	*Sunan*
Fifth Century AH		

al-Hakim al-Nishapuri	405	*Ilzamat* work. *Al-Mustadrak.* Ilzamat (addendum) works identify hadiths not in the Sahihan but of the same high authenticity standard
Abu Dharr al-Harawi	356–434	*Ilzamat* work
al-Bayhaqi	460	*Sunan al-Kubr*

Notes

[1] Collections containing traditions on the collection of the Quran by Abu Bakr or by Uthman analysed for their authenticity by Harald Motzki. His results are summarised in Chapter 6. Motzki also analysed relevant traditions recorded in works by Musa b. Uqba and Ibn Shabba (listed in ANNEX 3) and Abu Ubayd and Ibn Abu Dawud (listed in ANNEX 2). In total Motzki analysed 34 traditions.

ANNEX 2 – Early Muslim Literature – Works Concerning the Quran

ANNEX 2 gives an extended list of the types of works mentioned in Chapter 8, Early Muslim Literature, that mention or examine Quranic variants. It covers works concerning the interpretation (*tafsir*) and meaning of the Quran and works about the meaning of unusual words and the correct understanding of the grammar of the Quran.

Tafsir and Other Works Concerning the Quran (Also showing sources used by Arthur Jeffery in his book *Materials for the History of the Text of the Quran*)		
Author	**Lifetime or Year Died AH**	**Notable Works**
Ibn Amir al-Yahsubi [2]	118	[NLE] *Ikhtilaf masahif al-Sham wa l-Hidjaz wa l-Irak (Discrepancies between the Manuscripts of Syria, the Hijaz, and Iraq)*
Second Century AH		
al-Kisai [2]	189	[NLE] *Ikhtilaf masahif ahl al-Madina wa-ahl al-Kufa wa-ahl al-Basra (Discrepancies between the Manuscripts of the People of Medina, Kufa, and Basra)*
al-Farra [1] [2]	207	*Maani al-Quran* / [NLE] *Ikhtilaf ahl al-Kufa wa l-Basra wa l-Sham fi l-masahif (Discrepancies of the People of Kufa, Basra, and Syria concerning the Manuscripts)*
Ibn Hisham [1]	218	*Mughni al-Labib* / *Tahdhib al-Tawadih*

Abu Ubayd	154–224	Kitab Fadail al-Quran (Excellent Qualities of the Holy Quran)
Third Century AH		
al-Madaini [2]	c. 231	[NLE] Ikhtilaf masahif wa-djam al-kiraat (Discrepancies between the manuscripts and the compiling of the Quran)
Ibn Qutayba	213–276	Tawil Mushkil al-Quran (The Interpretation of the Difficult Passages of the Quran) / Tafsir Gharib al-Quran / Gharib al-Hadith
al-Ṭabari [1]	224–310	Tafsir al-Quran (Commentary on the Quran)
Ibn Abi Dawud [1]	316	Kitab al-Masahif (Book of Quran Codices)
Ibn al-Mundhir	241–318	Tafsir Ibn al-Mundhir
Fourth CenturyAH		
Ibn Abi Hatim al-Razi	327	Tafsir al-Musnad / Tafsir al-Quran al-azim
Ibn al-Anbari [1] [2]	328	Kitab al-Insaf / [NLE] Kitab al-Masahif (Book of Quran Codices)
Abu Mansur al-Maturidi	239–332	Tawilat al-Quran (Book of the Interpretations of the Quran)
Ibn Ashta al-Isfahani [2]	360	[NLE] Kitab al-Masahif (Book of Quran Codices)
al-Jassas	370	Ahkam al-Quran (The Commands of the Quran)
Ibn Khalawayh [1]	370	Mukhtasar
Ibn Jinni [1]	392	Muhtasab
Fifth Century AH		

al-Thalabi	427	*Tafsir al-Thalabi*
al-Dani	371–444	*al-Muqni fi Rasm masahif al-Amsar*
al-Mawardi	450	*An-Nukat wa-l-Uyoon*
al-Qushayri	376–465	*Lataif al-Isharat al-Tafsir al-Quran*
al-Baghawi [1]	510	*Maalim at-Tansil*
Sixth Century AH		
al-Zamakhshari [1]	538	*al-Kashshaf (The Revealer)*
al-Tabarsi [1]	468–584	*Majma al-Bayan fi Ulum al-Quran*
Ibn al-Jawzi	597	
Fakhr al-Din al-Razi [1]	544–606	*Tafsir al-Kabir (The Large Commentary)*
al-Ukbari [1]	538–616	*al-Tibyan fi irab al-Quran (The elucidation of the semantic grammar of the Quran)*
Seventh Century AH and After		
al-Qurtubi [1]	671	*al-Jami li Ahkam al-Quran*
al-Baydawi [1]	685	*Anwar al-Tansil wa Asrar al-Tawil (The Lights of Revelation and the Secrets of Interpretation)*
Abu l-Barakat al-Nasafi [1]	710	*Madarik al-Tanzil wa Haqaiq al-Tawil*
Ibn Manzur [1]	630–712	*Lisan al-Arab*
Nizam al-Din al-Nisaburi [1]	After 729	*Gharaib al-Quran wa-raghaib al-furqan (Wonders of the Quran and desirable features of revelation)*
Abu Hayyan al-Gharnati [1]	654–745	*Tafsir al-Bahr al-Muhit (The Explanation Ocean; Commentary on the linguistic meanings of the Quran).*
al-Suyuti [1]	849–911	*al-Itqan fi Ulum al-Quran (Perfect*

		Guide to the Sciences of the Quran) / al-Durr al-Manthur fi al-Tafsir al-Mathur / al-Muzhir (Linguistics)
Muttaqi al-Hindi [1]	888–975	Kanz al-Ummal

Notes

[1] Authors of works used as sources by Arthur Jeffery in his book *Materials for the History of the Text of the Quran*.

[2] Authors of works listed by al-Nadim (d. 384 AH), a famous Muslim librarian who made a catalogue, *The Fihrist*, of all the books in Arabic in the year 375 AH, as covering "Discrepancies of the Quranic Manuscripts" and of "Quran codices", but no longer exist.

[NLE] Work no longer exists.

ANNEX 3 – Early Muslim Literature – History

This ANNEX covers another important category of Muslim literature that provides information about the society and environment in which the Quran was collected and codified. It includes the *sira* works that tell us about the life of the Prophet, and the *maghazi* works, about the battles and campaigns that spread Islam throughout the Middle East. This is not a complete list. There are at least in the order of three times as many historians as shown here.

The most famous work is Ibn Ishaq's biography of the Prophet, *Sirat Rasul Allah*, which no longer exists but is found in edited form in other works such as Ibn Hisham's *Sirat Sayyidina Muhammad Rasul Allah*.

Historical Works - *Sira* and *Maghazi*		
Historians	**Lifetime or Year Died AH**	**Notable Works**
al-Zubayr [1]	23–94	Major transmitter of traditions
Aban b. Uthman b. Affan	c.105	
Wahb b. Munabbih	34–c.114	
Second Century AH		
al-Zuhri [2]	c.50–124	Major transmitter of traditions
Musa b. Uqbah	141	[NLE] *Kitab al-Maghazi (The Book of Expeditions)*
Ibn Ishaq	150	[NLE] *Sirat Rasul Allah (Life of the Messenger of God)*
Mamar b. Rashid al-Azdi [3]	153	Major transmitter of traditions

Abu Mikhnaf	157	
Sayf b. Umar al-Usayyidi al-Tamimi	c.180	*Kitab al-ridda wa l-futuh*
Hisham b. al-Kalbi	204	
al-Haytham b. Adi	c.207	
al-Waqidi	130–207	*Kitab al-Tarikh wa al-Maghazi (Book of History and Campaigns)*
Third Century AH		
Ibn Hisham	218	*Sirat Sayyidina Muhammad Rasul Allah (The life of Muhammad the Messenger of God).* Contains an edited version of Ibn Ishaq's *Sirat Rasul Allah*
Ibn Sa'd	168–230	*Kitab al-Tabaqat al-Kubra (Book of the Major Classes).* Also contains biographies of Companions
al-Madaini	c.231	
Khalifa b. Khayyat	240	*Kitab al-Tarikh / Kitab al-Tabaqat*
Ibn Abd al-Hakam	187–257	*Futuh Misr wal-Maghrib wa akhbaruha*
Umar b. Shabba	264	*Tarikh al-Madinah al-Munawwarah*
Ibn Qutayba	213–276	*Uyun al-Akhbar / Kitab al-Maarif*
al-Baladhuri	279	*Ansab al-Ashraf (Lineage of the Nobles) / Kitab Futuh al-Buldan (Book of the Conquests of Lands)*
al-Dinawari	282	*al-Akhbar al-tiwal*

al-Yaqubi	284	
al-Tabari	224–310	*Tarikh al-Rusul wa al-Muluk (History of the Prophets and Kings).* Contains edited part of Ibn Ishaq's *Sirat Rasul Allah*
Ibn Atham al-Kufi	314	*Kitab al-Futuh*
Fourth Century AH and after		
al-Masudi	345	*Kitab al-Tanbih wa l-ishraf*
Thabit b. Sinan al-Sabi	365/366	*Tuhfat al-umara fi tarikh al wuzara*
Ibn Miskawayh	421/422	
al-Utbi	427/428	
Hilal b. al-Muhassin al-Sabi	447/448	
al-Khatib al-Baghdadi	392–463	*al-Jami li-akhlaq al-rawi wa-adab al-sami*
Abu Ishaq al-Shirazi	475/476	

Notes

[1] Urwa b. al-Zubayr was a grandson of Abu Bakr, the first caliph, and thus a nephew of Aisha, Muhammad's youngest wife. His older brother was Abdullah b. al-Zubayr who set-up a rival caliphate to the Umayyads but was eventually defeated and killed in the first civil war. Thousands of traditions go back to Urwa who is believed to be the first collector and transmitter of biographical material about Muhammad. His reports are not contemporary accounts but living in the late first century he was in a position to question contemporaries of the Prophet and eye-witnesses of events 35 to 70 years after the Prophet's death.

[2] Ibn Shihab al-Zuhri is one of the first systematic collectors and teachers of traditions concerning Muhammad and his name occurs frequently in the *isnads* of such traditions. He is regarded as one of

the greatest Sunni authorities on Hadith. He was a prominent member of the Umayyad court from the time of caliph Abd al-Malik (r. 65–86 AH) to that of Hisham (r. 105–125 AH). Chapter 6 includes a summary of a modern analysis of some of his traditions concerning the collection of the Quran.

[3] Mamar b. Rashid al-Azdi transmitted one of the earliest accounts of Muhammad's life which forms a large part of the traditions collection of his student Abd al-Razzaq, listed in ANNEX 1.

[NLE] Work no longer exists.

ANNEX 4 – Timeline

The timeline is in years AH because years AH, starting at 1, make it easier to comprehend the overall timescale of the matters described in this book.

Table 8 at the end of this ANNEX gives a framework for converting AH years to CE years for the timeline given below and for other AH and CE dates mentioned in the book.

The Timeline is divided into four columns. The first column, from the left, covers political and religious figures, the second covers authors of tradition collections and Quran commentaries, the third covers historians, and the fourth mentions major historical events.

AH			
10	Abu-Bakr r. 11–13		
20	Umar r. 13–24		Conquest of Syria, Persia and Egypt 16-22
30	Uthman r. 24–35		
40	Ali ibn Abi Talib 40		First Civil War 36-41
50	Aisha 58		Umayyad Dynasty Established
60			
70			Second Civil War 60-73
80	Abd al-Malik r. 65–86		Conquest of Spain, Sind, Transoxonia
90	Al-Hajjaj g. 75–95	al-Zubayr 23–94	92
100			
110			Battle of Tours 114
120			
130		al-Zuhri 124	End of Umayyad Rule 132
140			New Abbasid Dynasty make Bagdad capital 145
150		Ibn Ishaq 150	
160			
170			

AH			
	Malik ibn Anas 93–179		
180			
190	Hurun al-Rashid r. 170–193		
200		al-Farra 207	
210	al-Razzaq 126–211		
220		Ibn Hisham 218	Conquest of Sicily and Southern Italy 225
230		Ibn Sa'd 168–230	
240	Ibn Hanbal 164–241		
250		al-Kindi 252	
260	al-Bukhari 194–256		
270	Muslim 204–261		
280	al-Tirmidi 209–279	Ibn Qutayba 213–276	
290			Foundation of Fatimid Dynasty in North Africa 297
300	al-Tabari 224–310		
310	Ibn Abi Dawud 316		
320	Ibn Mujahid 245–323		
330			
340			

Table 8 – Years AH-CE Conversions

AH	CE	AH	CE
00	622	300	912 / 913
10	631 / 632	310	922 / 923
20	641	320	932 / 933
30	650 / 651	330	941 / 942
40	660 / 661	340	951 / 952
50	670 / 671	350	961 / 962
60	680	360	970 / 971
70	689 / 690	370	980 / 981
80	699 / 700	380	990 / 991
90	709	390	999 / 1000
100	718 / 719	400	1009 / 1010
110	728 / 729	410	1019 / 1020
120	738	420	1029
130	747 / 748	430	1038 / 1039
140	757 / 758	440	1048 / 1049
150	767 / 768	450	1058 / 1059
160	776 / 777	460	1067 / 1068
170	786 / 787	470	1077 / 1078
180	796 / 797	480	1087 / 1088
190	805 / 806	490	1096 / 1097
200	815 / 816	500	1106 / 1107
210	825 / 826	510	1116 / 1117
220	835	520	1126 / 1127
230	844 / 845	530	1135 / 1136
240	854 / 855	540	1145 / 1146
250	864 / 865	550	1154 / 1156
260	874	560	1164 / 1165

270	883 / 884	570	1174 / 1175
280	893 / 894	580	1184 / 1185
290	903	590	1194
		600	1203 / 1204

Notes

Chapter 1 – Introduction

[1] Hossein Modarressi, *Early Debates on the Integrity of the Quran: A Brief Survey*, Studia Islamica, No. 77 (1993), pp5-39, p8

Gregor Schoeler, *The Codification of the Quran: A Comment on the Hypotheses of Burton and Wansbrough* in *The Quran in Context: Historical and Literary Investigations Into the Quranic Milieu*, Brill Academic Publishers, 2009, p784

[2] Michael Cook, *Muhammad (Past Masters)*, Oxford University Press, 1983, 1999, Chp. 7, L691

Herbert Berg, *Collection and Canonization of the Quran*, in *Routledge Handbook on Early Islam*, Routledge, 2017, L1508

[3] Harold Motzki, *Alternative Accounts of the Qurans Formation*, in *The Cambridge Companion to the Quran*, Cambridge University Press, 2006, p59

[4] Nicolai Sinai, *When did the consonantal skeleton of the Quran reach closure?* Bulletin of the School of Oriental and African Studies 77 (2014), p3

Chapter 2 – The Abu Bakr Collection

[1] Theodor Nöldeke, Friedrich Schwally, Gotthelf Bergsträsser, Otto Pretzl, *The History of the Quran*, Brill, 1937, p229 (ii/20)

W. Montgomery Watt and Richard L. Bell, *Introduction to the Quran*, Edinburgh University Press, 1970, 1995, Chp. 3, L903

[2] Theodor Nöldeke, Friedrich Schwally, Gotthelf Bergsträsser, Otto Pretzl, *The History of the Quran*, Brill, 1937, p230 (ii/20)

W. Montgomery Watt and Richard L. Bell, *Introduction to the Quran*, Edinburgh University Press, 1970, 1995, Chp. 3, L915

[3] W. Montgomery Watt and Richard L. Bell, *Introduction to the Quran*, Edinburgh University Press, 1970, 1995, Chp. 3, L915

[4] Ibid., Chp. 3, L927

[5] Herbert Berg, *Collection and Canonization of the Quran*, in *Routledge Handbook on Early Islam*, Routledge, 2017, L1441. Berg reference: Ibn Abi Dawud, Masahif, 16

Alford T. Welch, *History of the Quran after 632*, in *The Quran*, in *Encyclopaedia of Islam*, Second Edition, Brill. Welch reference: Ibn Abi Dawud, Masahif, 10; Itqan, i, 58

[6] Alford T. Welch, *History of the Quran after 632*, in *The Quran*, in *Encyclopaedia of Islam*, Second Edition, Brill. Welch reference: Ibn Saʿd, iii/1, 212

[7] Theodor Nöldeke, Friedrich Schwally, Gotthelf Bergsträsser, Otto Pretzl, *The History of the Quran*, Brill, 1937, p226 (ii/15)

[8] Alford T. Welch, *History of the Quran after 632*, in *The Quran*, in *Encyclopaedia of Islam*, Second Edition, Brill. Welch references: Ibn Abi Dawud, Masahif, 10; Itqan, i, 57-9

[9] Hossein Modarressi, *Early Debates on the Integrity of the Quran: A Brief Survey*, Studia Islamica, No. 77 (1993), pp5-39, p14. Modarressi references: Ibn Asakir, biography of Uthman, p170; Zarkashi, I, p241; Itqan, I, p248

[10] Alford T. Welch, *History of the Quran after 632*, in *The Quran*, in *Encyclopaedia of Islam*, Second Edition, Brill

[11] Harald Motzki, *The Collection of the Quran A Reconsideration of Western Views in Light of Recent Methodological Developments*, Der Islam, Vol. 78, Issue 1, pp1-34, 2001, p8

[12] A. Jones, *The History of the Text of the Quran after the Death of Muhammad*, in *The Quran II*, in *Arabic Literature to the End of the Umayyad Period*, Cambridge University Press, 1983, 2010, p237

Gregor Schoeler, *The Codification of the Quran: A Comment on the Hypotheses of Burton and Wansbrough* in *The Quran in Context:*

Historical and Literary Investigations Into the Quranic Milieu, Brill
Academic Publishers, 2009, p784

Chapter 3 – Companion Codices

[1] Behnam Sadeghi, *Origins of the Koran: From revelation to holy
book*, BBC, 2015 https://www.bbc.co.uk/news/world-middle-
east-33631745

Samuel Green, *Chapter 6: How many collections of the Quran were
made by the companions of Muhammad?* in *The Preservation Of The
Quran - An Examination Of The Common Claims Made About The
Quran*, 2017
http://engagingwithislam.org/leaflets/Preservation_Quran.pdf

[2] A. Jones, *The History of the Text of the Quran after the Death of
Muhammad*, in *The Quran II*, in *Arabic Literature to the End of the
Umayyad Period*, Cambridge University Press, 1983, 2010, p238

Claude Gilliot, *Creation of a Fixed Text* in *The Cambridge
Companion to the Quran*, Cambridge University Press, 2006, p47

[3] Arthur Jeffery, *Materials for the History of the Text of the Quran:
The Old Codices*, E.J. Brill, 1937, p14

Alford T. Welch, *History of the Quran after 632*, in *The Quran*, in
Encyclopaedia of Islam, Second Edition, Brill

[4] Herbert Berg, *Collection and Canonization of the Quran*, in
Routledge Handbook on Early Islam, Routledge, 2017, L1475. Berg
reference: Ibn Abi Shayba, VII, p204

[5] John Gilchrist, *Chapter 3: The Codices of Ibn Mas'ud and Ubayy b.
Ka'b*, in *The Codification of the Quran Text*, Answering Islam,
1989. Gilchrist reference: Ibn Sa'd, Kitab al-Tabaqat al-Kabir,
Vol. 2, p441 https://www.answering-
islam.org/Gilchrist/Jam/chap3.html

[6] Theodor Nöldeke, Friedrich Schwally, Gotthelf Bergsträsser,
Otto Pretzl, *The History of the Quran*, Brill, 1937, p219 (ii/8)

[7] Alford T. Welch, *History of the Quran after 632*, in *The Quran*, in *Encyclopaedia of Islam*, Second Edition, Brill. Welch reference: e.g. Ibn al-Nadim, Fihrist, 28; tr. Dodge, 62f

[8] Arzina R. Lalani, *Ali b. Abi Talib*, in *The Quran: An Encyclopedia*, Routledge, 2005, p30. Lalani references: Ibn Sa'd's Tabaqat; al-Baladhuri's Ansab; al- Suyuti's Itqan

[9] Hossein Modarressi, *Early Debates on the Integrity of the Quran: A Brief Survey*, Studia Islamica, No. 77 (1993), pp5-39, p18, Note 73. Modarressi reference: Itqan, I, p204

[10] Ahmed el-Wakil, *New Light on the Collection and Authenticity of the Quran: The Case for the Existence of a 'Master Copy'*, Journal of Shi'a Islamic Studies, Vol. 8, Number 4, 2015, pp409-448. el-Wakil references: al-Suyuti, Itqan; al-Hakim al-Haskani, Shawahid al-Tanzil; Ibn Ishaq; al-Nadim.

[11] Hossein Modarressi, *Early Debates on the Integrity of the Quran: A Brief Survey*, Studia Islamica, No. 77 (1993), pp5-39, pp17-18, Note 71. Modarressi references: Ibn Sa'd, II (2), p101; Ibn Abi Shayba, VI, p148; Abu Hilal al-Askari, I, pp219-20; Ibn Abi Dawud, p10; Itqan, I, p204

[12] Arthur Jeffery, *Materials for the History of the Text of the Quran: The Old Codices*, E.J. Brill, 1937

Chapter 4 – Uthman

[1] Alford T. Welch, *History of the Quran after 632*, in *The Quran*, in *Encyclopaedia of Islam*, Second Edition, Brill

Claude Gilliot, *Creation of a Fixed Text*, in *The Cambridge Companion to the Quran*, Cambridge University Press, 2006, p45

A. Jones, *The History of the Text of the Quran after the Death of Muhammad*, in *The Quran II*, in *Arabic Literature to the End of the Umayyad Period*, Cambridge University Press, 1983, 2010, p239

[2] Claude Gilliot, *Creation of a Fixed Text*, in *The Cambridge Companion to the Quran*, Cambridge University Press, 2006, p45

[3] Theodor Nöldeke, Friedrich Schwally, Gotthelf Bergsträsser, Otto Pretzl, *The History of the Quran*, Brill, 1937, pp259-262 (ii/57-62)

Alford T. Welch, *History of the Quran after 632*, in *The Quran*, in *Encyclopaedia of Islam*, Second Edition, Brill

[4] James White, *What Every Christian Needs to Know About the Quran*, Bethany House, 2013, Chp. 11, L3442

[5] W. Montgomery Watt and Richard L. Bell, *Introduction to the Quran*, Edinburgh University Press, 1970, 1995, Chp. 3, L951

John Gilchrist, *Chapter 2: The Uthmanic Recension of the Quran*, in *Codification of the Quran Text*, Answering Islam, 1989 https://www.answering-islam.org/Gilchrist/Jam/chap2.html

[6] John Burton, *The Collection of the Quran*, Cambridge University Press, 1977, p142. Burton reference: Ibn Abi Dawud, Masahif, p11

[7] Ibid., p143. Burton Reference: Ibn Abi Dawud, Masahif, p21

[8] Ibid., p145. Burton Reference: Ibn Abi Dawud, Masahif, pp23-4

[9] Ibid., p123. Burton reference: Ibn Abi Dawud, Masahif, p10

[10] Ibid., p146. Burton reference: Ibn Abi Dawud, Masahif, p13

[11] Gregor Schoeler, *The Codification of the Quran: A Comment on the Hypotheses of Burton and Wansbrough* in *The Quran in Context: Historical and Literary Investigations Into the Quranic Milieu*, Brill Academic Publishers, 2009, p787

[12] Ibid., p787. Schoeler reference: al-Tabari, Tarikh, Vol. 1, 2952

[13] Ibid., p787. Schoeler reference: al-Baladhuri, Ansab, Vol. 4.1, 550ff

[14] Ibid., p787. Schoeler reference: Ibn Abi Dawud, Masahif, 12

[15] Behnam Sadeghi and Uwe Bergmann, *The codex of the companion of the Prophet and the Quran of the Prophet*, Arabica 57 (2010), pp364-366

[16] Arthur Jeffery, *Materials for the History of the Text of the Quran: The Old Codices*, E.J. Brill, 1937, p8

[17] Samuel Green, *Chapter 8: Did all of the companions of the Muhammad agree with Uthman's actions?* in *The Preservation Of The Quran - An Examination Of The Common Claims Made About The Quran*, 2017. Green references: Sunan al-Tirmidhi, Vol. 4, no. 3105, p134; Ibn Sa'd, Kitab al-Tabaqat al-Kabir, Vol. 2, p444 https://www.answering-islam.org/Green/uthman.htm

[18] John Gilchrist, *Chapter 3: The Codices of Ibn Mas'ud and Ubayy b. Ka'b*, in *The Codification of the Quran Text*, Answering Islam, 1989. Gilchrist reference: Ibn Sa'd, Kitab al-Tabaqat al-Kabir, Vol. 2, p444 https://www.answering-islam.org/Gilchrist/Jam/chap3.html

[19] John Burton, *The Collection of the Quran*, Cambridge University Press, 1977, p167. Burton reference: Ibn Abi Dawud, Masahif, p35

Chapter 5 – Variants

[1] Yasin Dutton, *Orality, Literacy and the Seven Ahruf Hadith*, Journal of Islamic Studies 23:1 (2012) pp1–49

[2] Fred M. Donner, *The Quran In Recent Scholarship*, in *The Quran in its Historical Context*, Routledge, 2008

[3] Adam Bursi, *Connecting the Dots: Diacritics, Scribal Culture, and the Quran in the First/Seventh Century*, Journal of the International Quranic Studies Association, Vol. 3 (2018), pp111-157

[4] Alford T. Welch, *History of the Quran after 632*, in *The Quran, in Encyclopaedia of Islam*, Second Edition, Brill

W. Montgomery Watt and Richard L. Bell, *Introduction to the Quran*, Edinburgh University Press, 1970, 1995, Chp. 3, L1021

James A. Bellamy, *Textual Criticism of the Quran*, in *Encyclopaedia of the Quran*, Brill

Behnam Sadeghi, *Origins of the Koran: From revelation to holy book*, BBC, 2015 https://www.bbc.co.uk/news/world-middle-east-33631745

Wikipedia, *Defective script*
https://en.wikipedia.org/wiki/Defective_script

[5] Frederik Leemhuis, *Readings of the Quran*, in *Encyclopaedia of the Quran*, Brill

John Burton, *The Collection of the Quran*, Cambridge University Press, 1977, p148

John Gilchrist, *Chapter 5: The Seven Different Readings*, in *The Codification of the Quran Text*, Answering Islam, 1989
https://www.answering-islam.org/Gilchrist/Jam/chap5.html

Behnam Sadeghi, *Origins of the Koran: From revelation to holy book*, BBC, 2015 https://www.bbc.co.uk/news/world-middle-east-33631745

[6] Gabriel Said Reynolds, *The Emergence of Islam: Classical Traditions in Contemporary Perspective*, Fortress Press, 2012, L2261

Arthur Jeffery, *Materials for the History of the Text of the Quran: The Old Codices*, E.J. Brill, 1937, p8

Frederik Leemhuis, *Readings of the Quran*, in *Encyclopaedia of the Quran*, Brill

[7] Claude Gilliot, *Creation of a Fixed Text* in *The Cambridge Companion to the Quran*, Cambridge University Press, 2006, p47

Theodor Nöldeke, Friedrich Schwally, Gotthelf Bergsträsser, Otto Pretzl, *The History of the Quran*, Brill, 1937, pp392-402 (iii/6-iii/19)

[8] Alford T. Welch, *History of the Quran after 632*, in *The Quran*, in *Encyclopaedia of Islam*, Second Edition, Brill

Herbert Berg, *Collection and Canonization of the Quran*, in *Routledge Handbook on Early Islam*, Routledge, 2017, L1568

Chapter 6 – Reliability of Traditions

[1] Harald Motzki (Editor), *Hadith: Origins and Developments*, Routledge, 2004, 2016

Jonathan A. C. Brown, *Hadith (The Foundations of Islam)*, Oneworld Publications, 2017

Alan Paton, *Hadith: What, Why, and When....*, Parkhill Books, 2018

[2] Jonathan A. C. Brown, *Hadith: Muhammad's Legacy in the Medieval and Modern World*, Oneworld Publications, 2009, p69, L1516

[3] Alan Paton, *Hadith: What, Why, and When....*, Parkhill Books, 2018, pp89-95, L1305

[4] Harald Motzki, *The Collection of the Quran - A Reconsideration of Western Views in Light of Recent Methodological Developments*, Der Islam, Vol. 78, Issue 1, pp1-34, 2001

[5] John Wansbrough, *Quranic Studies: Sources and Methods of Scriptural Interpretation*, Prometheus Books, 1977, 2004 and *Sectarian Milieu: Content and Composition of Islamic Salvation History*, Prometheus Books, 1978, 2006

[6] Stephen J. Shoemaker, *The Death of a Prophet: The End of Muhammad's Life and the Beginnings of Islam*, University of Pennsylvania Press, 2011, p148

Nicolai Sinai, *When did the consonantal skeleton of the Quran reach closure?* Bulletin of the School of Oriental and African Studies 77, 2014, p4

Herbert Berg, *The Devine Sources*, in *The Ashgate Research Companion to Islamic Law*, Ashgate, 2014

Chapter 7 – Early Writing and Compilation

[1] John Gilchrist, *Chapter 1: The Initial Collection of the Quran Text*, in *The Codification of the Quran Text*, Answering Islam, 1989. Gilchrist reference: al-Suyuti, Itqan, p96
https://www.answering-islam.org/Gilchrist/Jam/chap1.html

W. Montgomery Watt and Richard L. Bell, *Introduction to the Quran*, Edinburgh University Press, 1970, 1995, Chp. 6, L2119

[2] A. Jones, *The Quran in Muhammad's Lifetime*, in *The Quran II*, in *Arabic Literature to the End of the Umayyad Period*, Cambridge University Press, 1983, 2010, p232. Jones reference: al-Suyuti, Itqan, p141

[3] W. Montgomery Watt and Richard L. Bell, *Introduction to the Quran*, Edinburgh University Press, 1970, 1995, Chp. 2, L853. Montgomery Watt reference: Ibn Hisham, 226f

[4] A. Jones, *The Quran in Muhammad's Lifetime*, in *The Quran II*, in *Arabic Literature to the End of the Umayyad Period*, Cambridge University Press, 1983, 2010, p234-235. Jones reference: al-Zamakhshari gives his account in his comments on vi.93 with a brief reference on xxiii.14 itself.

W. Montgomery Watt and Richard L. Bell, *Introduction to the Quran*, Edinburgh University Press, 1970, 1995, Chp. 2, L866

[5] Gregor Schoeler, *The Codification of the Quran: A Comment on the Hypotheses of Burton and Wansbrough* in *The Quran in Context: Historical and Literary Investigations Into the Quranic Milieu*, Brill Academic Publishers, 2009, p781. Schoeler reference: Nöldeke, Vol 1, p45 (i/45)

[6] Ibid., p781. Schoeler references: Nöldeke, Vol. 1, p45 (i/45) and Vol. 1, p46 (i/46)(and n5)

[7] Ibid., p781. Schoeler reference: Nöldeke, Vol. 2, p28 (i/28)

[8] Ibid., p783

[9] Herbert Berg, *Collection and Canonization of the Quran*, in *Routledge Handbook on Early Islam*, Routledge, 2017, L1413

[10] W. Montgomery Watt and Richard L. Bell, *Introduction to the Quran*, Edinburgh University Press, 1970, 1995

[11] Herbert Berg, *Context: Muhammad*, in *Wiley Blackwell Companion to the Quran*, Wiley-Blackwell, 2006, 2017, p208. Berg reference: Bell 1937-9: I, vi

W. Montgomery Watt and Richard L. Bell, *Introduction to the Quran*, Edinburgh University Press, 1970, 1995, L2760

[12] Arthur Jeffery, *Materials for the History of the Text of the Quran: The Old Codices*, E.J. Brill, 1937, p5

Chapter 8 – Early Muslim Literature

[1] Alford T. Welch, *History of the Quran after 632*, in *The Quran*, in *Encyclopaedia of Islam*, Second Edition, Brill

Samuel Green, *Chapter 6: How many collections of the Quran were made by the companions of Muhammad?* in *The Preservation Of The Quran - An Examination Of The Common Claims Made About The Quran*, 2017
http://engagingwithislam.org/leaflets/Preservation_Quran.pdf

W. Montgomery Watt and Richard L. Bell, *Introduction to the Quran*, Edinburgh University Press, 1970, 1995, L974

Arthur Jeffery, *Materials for the History of the Text of the Quran: The Old Codices*, E.J. Brill, 1937, pp2-3, pp17-18

[2] Harald Motzki (Editor), *Hadith: Origins and Developments*, Routledge, 2004, 2016

Jonathan A. C. Brown, *Hadith (The Foundations of Islam)*, Oneworld Publications, 2017

Alan Paton, *Hadith: What, Why, and When....*, Parkhill Books, 2018

Chapter 9 – Companion Codices Compared

[1] Arthur Jeffery, *Materials for the History of the Text of the Quran: The Old Codices*, E.J. Brill, 1937

[2] Ibid., p.ix

[3] Ibid., p.x, p9

[4] Ibid., p9

Frederick M. Denny, *Exegesis and recitation: their development as classical forms of Quranic piety*, in *Transitions and Transformations in the History of Religions: Essays in Honor of Joseph M. Kitagawa*, Brill, 1980, p116

[5] Alford T. Welch, *History of the Quran after 632*, in *The Quran*, in *Encyclopaedia of Islam*, Second Edition, Brill

W. Montgomery Watt and Richard L. Bell, *Introduction to the Quran*, Edinburgh University Press, 1970, 1995, L999

[6] John Gilchrist, *Chapter 3: The Codices of Ibn Mas'ud and Ubayy b. Ka'b*, in *The Codification of the Quran Text*, Answering Islam, 1989. Gilchrist reference: al-Suyuti, Itqan, p186
https://www.answering-islam.org/Gilchrist/Jam/chap3.html

[7] Sean W. Anthony, *Two 'Lost' Suras of the Quran: Surat al-Khal and Surat al-Hafd between Textual and Ritual Canon*, JSAI 46 (2019)

Samuel Green, *Chapter 6: How many collections of the Quran were made by the companions of Muhammad?* in *The Preservation Of The Quran - An Examination Of The Common Claims Made About The Quran*, 2017, p10
http://engagingwithislam.org/leaflets/Preservation_Quran.pdf

John Gilchrist, *Chapter 3: The Codices of Ibn Mas'ud and Ubayy b. Ka'b*, in *The Codification of the Quran Text*, Answering Islam, 1989. Gilchrist reference: al-Suyuti, Itqan, p527
https://www.answering-islam.org/Gilchrist/Jam/chap3.html

[8] Alford T. Welch, *History of the Quran after 632*, in *The Quran*, in *Encyclopaedia of Islam*, Second Edition, Brill

A. Jones, *The History of the Text of the Quran after the Death of Muhammad*, in *The Quran II*, in *Arabic Literature to the End of the Umayyad Period*, Cambridge University Press, 1983, 2010, p239

[9] John Burton, *The Collection of the Quran*, Cambridge University Press, 1977, p142

[10] John Gilchrist, *Chapter 2: The Uthmanic Recension of the Quran*, in *The Codification of the Quran Text*, Answering Islam, 1989
https://www.answering-islam.org/Gilchrist/Jam/chap2.html

[11] John Gilchrist, *Chapter 3: The Codices of Ibn Mas'ud and Ubayy b. Ka'b*, in *The Codification of the Quran Text*, Answering Islam, 1989. Gilchrist references: Abu Ubayd's Kitab Fadail al-Quran; Nöldeke, 3.63; Jeffery, Materials, p31 https://www.answering-islam.org/Gilchrist/Jam/chap3.html

[12] John Gilchrist, *Chapter 4: The Missing Passages of the Quran*, in *The Codification of the Quran Text*, Answering Islam, 1989. Gilchrist reference: Jeffery, Materials, p32
https://www.answering-islam.org/Gilchrist/Jam/chap4.html

[13] Alford T. Welch, *History of the Quran after 632*, in *The Quran*, in *Encyclopaedia of Islam*, Second Edition, Brill

[14] John Gilchrist, *Chapter 3: The Codices of Ibn Mas'ud and Ubayy b. Ka'b*, in *The Codification of the Quran Text*, Answering Islam, 1989. Gilchrist references: Nöldeke 3.85; Jeffery, Materials, p128
https://www.answering-islam.org/Gilchrist/Jam/chap3.html

[15] Ibid., Gilchrist references: al-Tabari, 7.19.11; Nöldeke, 3.66 (iii/66); Jeffery, Materials, p40, p129. See link above

[16] Ibid., Gilchrist references: Maki's Kitab al-Kasf; Nöldeke, 3.66 (iii/66); Jeffery, Materials, p40, p129. See link above

[17] Ibid., Gilchrist references: al-Tabari, 8.60.16; Nöldeke, 3.66 (iii/66); Jeffery, Materials, p42. See link above

[18] Ibid., Gilchrist references: al-Tabari, 21.70.8; Nöldeke, 3.71 (iii/71); Jeffery, Materials, p75. This variant was likewise recorded in the codices of Ubayy b. Ka'b (Jeffery, Materials, p156). See link above

[19] Mondher Sfar, *In Search of the Original Koran: The True History of the Revealed Text*, Prometheus Books, 2008, L179

[20] David S. Powers, *Sinless, Sonless and Seal of Prophets: Muhammad and Quran 33, 36-40, Revisited*, Arabica 67:4 (2020)

Devin Stewart and Gabriel Said Reynolds, *Afterword: The Academic Study of the Quran - Achievements, Challenges, and Prospects*, JIQSA 1 (2016), pp173–183, p174

[21] Mondher Sfar, *In Search of the Original Koran: The True History of the Revealed Text*, Prometheus Books, 2008, L197

[22] Ibid., L162

[23] John Gilchrist, *Chapter 3: The Codices of Ibn Mas'ud and Ubayy b. Ka'b*, in *The Codification of the Quran Text*, Answering Islam, 1989. Gilchrist references: Fihrist S.26 Z.26; Nöldeke 3.77 (iii/77); Jeffery, Materials, p113 and p180 https://www.answering-islam.org/Gilchrist/Jam/chap3.html

Chapter 10 – Suras and Verses

[1] A. Jones, *The History of the Text of the Quran after the Death of Muhammad*, in *The Quran II*, in *Arabic Literature to the End of the Umayyad Period*, Cambridge University Press, 1983, 2010, pp238-239

Herbert Berg, *Collection and Canonization of the Quran*, in *Routledge Handbook on Early Islam*, Routledge, 2017, L1492

John Gilchrist, *Chapter 4: The Missing Passages of the Quran*, in *The Codification of the Quran Text*, Answering Islam, 1989. Gilchrist reference: Muslim, Vol. 2, p501
https://www.answering-islam.org/Gilchrist/Jam/chap4.html

Hossein Modarressi, *Early Debates on the Integrity of the Quran: A Brief Survey*, Studia Islamica, No. 77 (1993), pp5-39, p12

[2] John Gilchrist, *Chapter 4: The Missing Passages of the Quran*, in *The Codification of the Quran Text*, Answering Islam, 1989. Gilchrist reference: al-Suyuti, Itqan, p525
https://www.answering-islam.org/Gilchrist/Jam/chap4.html

[3] Luke Wayne, *Have there been changes to the Quran?* 2016
https://carm.org/have-there-been-changes-in-the-quran

Keith Thompson, *Lost and forgotten Parts of the Koran*, in *The Corruption of the Koran: Evidence and New Research*, Exegetical Apologetics, 2018. Thompson reference: al-Bukhari, Vol. 8, Book 82, Hadith 817
http://www.exegeticalapologetics.com/2018/05/the-corruption-of-koran-evidence-and.html

John Gilchrist, *Chapter 4: The Missing Passages of the Quran*, in *The Codification of the Quran Text*, Answering Islam, 1989. Gilchrist reference: al-Bukhari, Vol. 8, p539
https://www.answering-islam.org/Gilchrist/Jam/chap4.html

[4] WikiIslam, the online resource on Islam. Reference: al-Muttaqi Ali bin Husam al-Din in his book Mukhtasar Kanz al-Ummal printed on the margin of Musnad Ahmad b. Hanbal, Vol. 2, p2, in his hadith about chapter 33
https://wikiislam.net/wiki/Corruption_of_the_Quran#The_lost_verse_on_stoning

https://wikiislam.net/wiki/Corruption_of_the_Quran#cite_note-36

[5] Hossein Modarressi, *Early Debates on the Integrity of the Quran: A Brief Survey*, Studia Islamica, No. 77 (1993), pp5-39, p10.

Modarressi References: (Umar could not find two witnesses) Itqan, I, p206 / (Later recall) Ahmad, V, p183; Abd al-Razzaq, al-Musannaf, VII, p330; Itqan, III, p82, p86

[6] WikiIslam, the online resource on Islam. Reference: Musnad Ahmad b. Hanbal, 21245
https://wikiislam.net/wiki/Corruption_of_the_Quran#Most_of_Surah_al-Ahzab_was_lost

[7] Ibid., Reference: Tafsir al Qurtubi, introduction for Surah Ahzab
https://wikiislam.net/wiki/Corruption_of_the_Quran#Most_of_Surah_al-Ahzab_was_lost

[8] Hossein Modarressi, *Early Debates on the Integrity of the Quran: A Brief Survey*, Studia Islamica, No. 77 (1993), pp5-39, p12. Modarressi reference: al-Suyuti, Durr, V, p180

[9] Keith Thompson, *Lost and forgotten Parts of the Koran*, in *The Corruption of the Koran: Evidence and New Research*, Exegetical Apologetics, 2018. Thompson reference: Muslim, Book 8, Hadith 3421 http://www.exegeticalapologetics.com/2018/05/the-corruption-of-koran-evidence-and.html

John Gilchrist, *Chapter 4: The Missing Passages of the Quran*, in *The Codification of the Quran Text*, Answering Islam, 1989. Gilchrist reference: Muslim, Vol. 2, p740
https://www.answering-islam.org/Gilchrist/Jam/chap4.html

[10] WikiIslam, the online resource on Islam. References: al-Suyuti, Itqan, Part 3, p184; Tafsir al-Qurtubi on Surah al Bara'at; al-Tirmidhi, Vol. 5, Book 44, Hadith 3086
https://wikiislam.net/wiki/Corruption_of_the_Quran#Lost_verses_from_Surah_at-Tawba

https://wikiislam.net/wiki/Corruption_of_the_Quran#cite_note-58

https://wikiislam.net/wiki/Corruption_of_the_Quran#cite_note-59

184

https://wikiislam.net/wiki/Corruption_of_the_Quran#cite_note-60

[11] Hossein Modarressi, *Early Debates on the Integrity of the Quran: A Brief Survey*, Studia Islamica, No. 77 (1993), pp5-39, p12. Modarressi references: (One-fourth) Hakim, II, p331; Haytami, Majma al-zawaid, VII, pp28-29; Itqan, III, p84 / (One-third) al-Suyuti, Durr, III, p208

[12] Ibid., Modarressi references: (Other verses) Mabani, p99; Itqan, III, p84 / (Duty to parents) Abd al-Razzaq, IX, p50; Ahmad, I, p47, p55; Ibn Abi Shayba, VII, p431; Bukhari, IV, p306; Ibn Salama, p22; Itqan, III, p84 / (Jihad) Muhasibi, p403; Mabani, p99; Itqan, III, p84 / (Three other Companions) Abd al-Razzaq, IX, p52; Muhasibi, p400; Itqan, III, p84

[13] Ibid., Modarressi references: Muhasibi, p399; Tabari, Jami', II, p479

[14] Ibid., Modarressi references: (Al-Ansari) Itqan, III, p84 / (Aisha) Abd al-Razzaq, VII, p470; Ibn Maja, I, pp625-626

[15] John Gilchrist, *Chapter 4: The Missing Passages of the Quran*, in *The Codification of the Quran Text*, Answering Islam, 1989. Gilchrist reference: al-Suyuti, Itqan, p524
https://www.answering-islam.org/Gilchrist/Jam/chap4.html

Hossein Modarressi, *Early Debates on the Integrity of the Quran: A Brief Survey*, Studia Islamica, No. 77 (1993), pp5-39, p11. Modarressi references: (Umar's son) Itqan, III, pp81-82 / (Other scholars) Ibn Abi Dawud, p23; Itqan, V, p179; Ibn Qutayba, Tawil, p313

[16] Neal Robinson, *Discovering the Quran: A Contemporary Approach to a Veiled Text*, Georgetown University Press, 1996, 2004, pp64-69

Wikipedia, *Naskh (tafsir)*
https://en.wikipedia.org/wiki/Naskh_(tafsir)

Nasr Abu Zayd, *Towards Understanding the Quran's Worldview*, in *New Perspectives on the Quran: The Quran in its Historical Context 2*, Routledge, 2011, 2014, L2153

W. Montgomery Watt and Richard L. Bell, *Introduction to the Quran*, Edinburgh University Press, 1970, 1995, L1754

Chapter 11 – Closure of the Quran

[1] Omar Hamdan, *The Second Masahif Project: A Step Towards the Canonization of the Quranic Text*, in *The Quran in Context: Historical and Literary Investigations Into the Quranic Milieu*, Brill Academic Publishers, 2009

[2] Nicolai Sinai, *When did the consonantal skeleton of the Quran reach closure?* Bulletin of the School of Oriental and African Studies 77 (2014), p6

Nicolai Sinai, *The Quran: A Historical-Critical Introduction*, Edinburgh University Press, 2017, p45

Stephen J. Shoemaker, *The Death of a Prophet: The End of Muhammad's Life and the Beginnings of Islam*, University of Pennsylvania Press, 2011, pp146-158

Fred M. Donner, *The Quran In Recent Scholarship*, in *The Quran in its Historical Context*, Routledge, 2008, L1357

Angelika Neuwirth, *Structure And Emergence Of Community*, in *Wiley Blackwell Companion to the Quran*, Wiley-Blackwell, 2006, 2017, p143

[3] Nicolai Sinai, *When did the consonantal skeleton of the Quran reach closure?* Bulletin of the School of Oriental and African Studies 77 (2014), p7

Stephen J. Shoemaker, *The Death of a Prophet: The End of Muhammad's Life and the Beginnings of Islam*, University of Pennsylvania Press, 2011, p148

[4] Estelle Whelan, *Forgotten Witness: Evidence For The Early Codification Of The Quran*, Journal of The American Oriental Society, 1998, Vol. 118, pp1-14

[5] Nicolai Sinai, *When did the consonantal skeleton of the Quran reach closure?* Bulletin of the School of Oriental and African Studies 77 (2014), p9

[6] Ibid., pp10-11

[7] Ibid., pp12-13

[8] Ibid., p14

[9] Stephen J. Shoemaker, *Muhammad And The Quran*, in *The Oxford Handbook of Late Antiquity*, OUP USA, 2012, p1088

Stephen J. Shoemaker, *The Death of a Prophet: The End of Muhammad's Life and the Beginnings of Islam*, University of Pennsylvania Press, 2011, p147

Herbert Berg, *The Devine Sources*, in *The Ashgate Research Companion to Islamic Law*, Ashgate, 2014, p35

[10] Gregor Schoeler, *The Codification of the Quran: A Comment on the Hypotheses of Burton and Wansbrough* in *The Quran in Context: Historical and Literary Investigations Into the Quranic Milieu*, Brill Academic Publishers, 2009, p788

Nicolai Sinai, *The Quran: A Historical-Critical Introduction*, Edinburgh University Press, 2017, pp46-47

Nicolai Sinai, *When did the consonantal skeleton of the Quran reach closure?* Bulletin of the School of Oriental and African Studies 77 (2014), p36

[11] Chase F. Robinson, *Abd al-Malik (Makers of the Muslim World)*, Oneworld Publications, 2005, L1318-1369

[12] Nicolai Sinai, *When did the consonantal skeleton of the Quran reach closure?* Bulletin of the School of Oriental and African Studies 77 (2014), p12

Steven Turner, *A review and investigation of 8th century Christian polemics against the Quran*, Arabic 5701, 2017

Chapter 12 – Indications in the Quran

[1] Harald Motzki (Editor), *Hadith: Origins and Developments*, Routledge, 2004, 2016

Jonathan A C Brown, *Hadith (The Foundations of Islam)*, Oneworld Publications, 2017

Alan Paton, *Hadith: What, Why, and When....*, Parkhill Books, 2018

[2] Fred M. Donner, *Narratives of Islamic Origins: The Beginnings of Islamic Historical Writing*, Darwin Press, 1998, pp35–61, p49

[3] Stephen J. Shoemaker, *The Death of a Prophet: The End of Muhammad's Life and the Beginnings of Islam*, University of Pennsylvania Press, 2011, p155

[4] Jonathan A C Brown, *Hadith (The Foundations of Islam)*, Oneworld Publications, 2017

Alan Paton, *Hadith: What, Why, and When....*, Parkhill Books, 2018, L164

[5] Stephen J. Shoemaker, *The Death of a Prophet: The End of Muhammad's Life and the Beginnings of Islam*, University of Pennsylvania Press, 2011, p153

[6] Nicolai Sinai, *When did the consonantal skeleton of the Quran reach closure?* Bulletin of the School of Oriental and African Studies 77 (2014), p44

[7] Stephen J. Shoemaker, *The Death of a Prophet: The End of Muhammad's Life and the Beginnings of Islam*, University of Pennsylvania Press, 2011, p156

[8] Nicolai Sinai, *The Quran: A Historical-Critical Introduction*, Edinburgh University Press, 2017, p48

[9] Nicolai Sinai, *When did the consonantal skeleton of the Quran reach closure?* Bulletin of the School of Oriental and African Studies 77 (2014), p45

[10] David S. Powers, *Muhammad Is Not the Father of Any of Your Men: The Making of the Last Prophet,* University of Pennsylvania Press, 2009, especially Chapter 4, pp35-71

[11] David S. Powers, *Zayd (Divinations: Rereading Late Ancient Religion),* University of Pennsylvania Press, 2014

[12] David S. Powers, *Sinless, Sonless and Seal of Prophets: Muhammad and Quran 33:36-40, Revisited,* Arabica 67:4 (2020)

[13] Nicolai Sinai, *The Quran: A Historical-Critical Introduction,* Edinburgh University Press, 2017, p52

[14] Tommaso Tesei, *'The Romans Will Win!' Q 30:2–7 in Light of 7th C. Political Eschatology,* Der Islam 2018; 95 (1): 1–29

Chapter 13 – Canonical Variant Readings

[1] Claude Gilliot, *Creation of a Fixed Text,* in *The Cambridge Companion to the Quran,* Cambridge University Press, 2006, p48

[2] W. Montgomery Watt and Richard L. Bell, *Introduction to the Quran,* Edinburgh University Press, 1970, 1995, L1056

A. Jones, *The History of the Text of the Quran after the Death of Muhammad,* in *The Quran II,* in *Arabic Literature to the End of the Umayyad Period,* Cambridge University Press, 1983, 2010, p244

Alford T. Welch, *History of the Quran after 632,* in *The Quran,* in *Encyclopaedia of Islam,* Second Edition, Brill

[3] W. Montgomery Watt and Richard L. Bell, *Introduction to the Quran,* Edinburgh University Press, 1970, 1995, L1056

[4] Arthur Jeffery, *Materials for the History of the Text of the Quran: The Old Codices,* E.J. Brill, 1937, p9

Frederick M. Denny, *Exegesis and recitation: their development as classical forms of Quranic piety,* in *Transitions and Transformations in the History of Religions: Essays in Honor of Joseph M. Kitagawa*, Brill, 1980, p116

[5] W. Montgomery Watt and Richard L. Bell, *Introduction to the Quran*, Edinburgh University Press, 1970, 1995, L1068

A. Jones, *The History of the Text of the Quran after the Death of Muhammad*, in *The Quran II*, in *Arabic Literature to the End of the Umayyad Period*, Cambridge University Press, 1983, 2010, p244

[6] Muhammad Mustafa al-Azami, *The History of the Quranic Text from Revelation to Compilation*, UK Islamic Academy, 2003, pp155–59

Ammar Khatib, Nazir Khan, *The Origins of the Variant Readings of the Quran*, Yaqeen Institute for Islamic Research, 2020 https://yaqeeninstitute.org/ammar-khatib/the-origins-of-the-variant-readings-of-the-quran

[7] Herbert Berg, *Collection and Canonization of the Quran*, in *Routledge Handbook on Early Islam*, Routledge, 2017, L1626

Christopher Melchert, *Ibn Mujahid and the Establishment of the Seven Quranic Readings*, Studia Islamica, 2000, no. 91, pp5-22

Christopher Melchert, *The Relation of the Ten Readings to One Another*, Journal of Quranic Studies, 2008, no. 10, pp73-87

[8] Yasin Dutton, *Orality, Literacy and the Seven Ahruf Hadith*, Journal of Islamic Studies 23:1 (2012) pp4-6

[9] Gabriel Said Reynolds, *Introduction: Quranic Studies and its Controversies*, in *The Quran in its Historical Context*, Routledge, 2007, L337

[10] Samuel Green, *Chapter 11: Are all Arabic Qurans used in the world today identical?* in *The Preservation Of The Quran - An Examination Of The Common Claims Made About The Quran*, 2017, p18 http://engagingwithislam.org/leaflets/Preservation_Quran.pdf

Chapter 14 – Extant Early Manuscripts

[1] Keith E. Small, *Textual Criticism and Quran Manuscripts*, Lexington, 2011, L144

Wikipedia, *Critical apparatus*
https://en.wikipedia.org/wiki/Critical_apparatus

[2] Gabriel Said Reynolds, *Introduction: Quranic Studies and its Controversies*, in *The Quran in its Historical Context*, Routledge, 2007, L351

Fred M. Donner, *The Study of Islams Origins Since W. Montgomery Watt's Publications*, Paper presented November 2015, at the University of Edinburgh, p31
https://www.scribd.com/document/360940402/The-Study-of-Islams-Origins-Since-W-Montgomery-Watt-s-Publications

Fred M. Donner, Review of *Textual Criticism and Quran Manuscripts* by Keith E. Small, *Journal of Near Eastern Studies* 73, no. 1 (April 2014): 166-169

[3] The Corpus Coranicum Project. Project Goals:
https://corpuscoranicum.de/
https://corpuscoranicum.de/about/index/sure/1/vers/1

The Corpus Coranicum Project. Manuscript Work:
https://corpuscoranicum.de/index/einleitung/sure/1/vers/2

The Corpus Coranicum Project. Manuscript Database:
https://corpuscoranicum.de/handschriften/uebersicht

[4] Keith E. Small, *Textual Criticism and Quran Manuscripts*, Lexington, 2011, L3450, and Note 45

[5] Ibid., L3629, Note 45. Sergio Noja-Noseda, Note Esterne in Margine Al 1 Volume *Dei Materiali per un Edizione Critica Del Corano, Rendiconti 134, 1:3-37.* Pages 19-28 contain a list of the contents of the known Hijazi manuscripts in the United States, European collections, the Middle East, and Istanbul.

[6] François Déroche, *Written Transmission*, in *Wiley Blackwell Companion to the Quran*, Wiley-Blackwell, 2017, p185

Daniel Alan Brubaker, *Corrections in Early Quran Manuscripts: Twenty Examples*, Think and Tell, 2019, Chp. 1, p18

[7] Tayyar Altikulaç, *Al-Mushaf al-Sharif attributed to Uthman bin Affan*, Research Centre For Islamic History, Art and Culture (IRCICA), 2007

François Déroche, Written Transmission, in Wiley Blackwell Companion to the Quran, Wiley-Blackwell, 2017, p185

Keith Thompson, *Dating the Uthmanic Manuscripts*, in *The Corruption of the Koran: Evidence and New Research*, Exegetical Apologetics, 2018
http://www.exegeticalapologetics.com/2018/05/the-corruption-of-koran-evidence-and.html

[8] Tayyar Altikulaç, *Al-Mushaf al-Sharif attributed to Uthman bin Affan*, Research Centre For Islamic History, Art and Culture (IRCICA), 2007, pp71-72

[9] Daniel Alan Brubaker, *Corrections in Early Quran Manuscripts: Twenty Examples*, Think and Tell, 2019, p4

[10] Ibid., p4

[11] Keith E. Small, *Textual Criticism and Quran Manuscripts*, Lexington, 2011, L222

Chapter 15 – Sanaa 1

[1] Islamic Awareness, *Codex Sanaa 1 – A Quranic Manuscript From Mid–1st Century Of Hijra - History Of The Manuscript*
https://www.islamic-awareness.org/quran/text/mss/soth

[2] Behnam Sadeghi and Mohsen Goudarzi, *Sanaa 1 and the Origins of the Quran*, Der Islam 87 (2012), 1-129, p10

[3] Ibid., p9

192

Wikipedia, *Sanaa manuscript*
https://en.wikipedia.org/wiki/Sanaa_manuscript#Restoration_p
roject

[4] Eleonore Cellard, Review of *The Sanaa Palimpsest: The Transmission of the Quran in the First Centuries AH by Asma Hilali*, Review of Quranic Research, Vol. 5, no. 9 (2019)

Behnam Sadeghi and Mohsen Goudarzi in *Sanaa 1 and the Origins of the Quran*, Der Islam 87 (2012), Table 3, pp37-39, lists the 35 folios from DAM 01-27.1 and the four auctioned folios that they studied.

[5] Islamic Awareness, *Codex Sanaa 1 – A Quranic Manuscript From Mid–1st Century Of Hijra - History Of The Manuscript*
https://www.islamic-awareness.org/quran/text/mss/soth

[6] Asma Hilali, *The Sanaa Palimpsest: The Transmission of the Quran in the First Centuries AH*, OUP/Institute of Ismaili Studies, (2017), pp13-14, p33

[7] Behnam Sadeghi and Mohsen Goudarzi, *Sanaa 1 and the Origins of the Quran*, Der Islam 87 (2012), 1-129, p11

Alba Fedeli, *Early Evidences of Variant Readings in Quranic Manuscripts*, in *The Hidden Origins of Islam: New Research into Its Early History*, Prometheus Books, 2008, pp311-344

[8] Behnam Sadeghi and Mohsen Goudarzi, *Sanaa 1 and the Origins of the Quran*, Der Islam 87 (2012), 1-129, p11

[9] Ibid., p12, p35

[10] Ibid., p12, p14

Fred M. Donner, *The Study of Islams Origins Since W. Montgomery Watt's Publications*, Paper presented November 2015, at the University of Edinburgh, p30
https://www.scribd.com/document/360940402/The-Study-of-Islams-Origins-Since-W-Montgomery-Watt-s-Publications

[11] Behnam Sadeghi and Uwe Bergmann, *The codex of the companion of the Prophet and the Quran of the Prophet*, Arabica 57 (2010), pp343-436

[12] Behnam Sadeghi and Mohsen Goudarzi, *Sanaa 1 and the Origins of the Quran*, Der Islam 87 (2012), 1-129

[13] These are estimates made by the present author using data from *Table 3. The Folios of Sanaa 1* in *Sanaa 1 and the Origins of the Quran*, Der Islam 87 (2012), p37

[14] Behnam Sadeghi and Mohsen Goudarzi, *Sana 1 and the Origins of the Quran*, Der Islam 87 (2012), 1-129

[15] Behnam Sadeghi and Uwe Bergmann, *The codex of the companion of the Prophet and the Quran of the Prophet*, Arabica 57 (2010), p348

[16] Ibid., p344

[17] Ibid., p345

[18] Ibid., p394

[19] Behnam Sadeghi and Mohsen Goudarzi, *Sanaa 1 and the Origins of the Quran*, Der Islam 87 (2012), p20

[20] Behnam Sadeghi and Uwe Bergmann, *The codex of the companion of the Prophet and the Quran of the Prophet*, Arabica 57 (2010), p344

[21] Behnam Sadeghi and Mohsen Goudarzi, *Sanaa 1 and the Origins of the Quran*, Der Islam 87 (2012), p22

[22] Behnam Sadeghi and Uwe Bergmann, *The codex of the companion of the Prophet and the Quran of the Prophet*, Arabica 57 (2010), p345

[23] The estimate of the number of verses is one made by the present author, using information given in Table 2, p355, of the Sadeghi and Bergmann 2010 paper and in Table 3, p37, of the

Sadeghi and Goudarzi 2012 paper. The numbers of major variants are given in Appendix 2, p422, of the 2010 paper.

[24] Behnam Sadeghi and Mohsen Goudarzi, *Sanaa 1 and the Origins of the Quran*, Der Islam 87 (2012), p21, Table 1

[25] Asma Hilali, *The Sanaa Palimpsest: The Transmission of the Quran in the First Centuries AH*, OUP/Institute of Ismaili Studies, (2017)

[26] Eleonore Cellard, Review of *The Sanaa Palimpsest: The Transmission of the Quran in the First Centuries AH by Asma Hilali*, Review of Quranic Research, Vol. 5, no. 9 (2019)

[27] Nicolai Sinai, *Beyond the Cairo Edition: On the Study of Early Quranic Codices*, Journal of the American Oriental Society 140.1 (2020)

[28] François Déroche, *Qurans of the Umayyads: A First Overview*, Brill (2013), p54

Chapter 16 – The Birmingham Quran

[1] Birmingham University, *The Birmingham Quran*
https://www.birmingham.ac.uk/facilities/cadbury/birmingham-quran-mingana-collection/birmingham-quran/index.aspx

Wikipedia, *Birmingham Quran manuscript*
https://en.wikipedia.org/wiki/Birmingham_Quran_manuscript

[2] Halim Sayoud, *Statistical Analysis of the Birmingham Quran Folios*, HDSKD journal, Vol. 4, No. 1, pp101-126, 2018, p102
http://scholarpage.org/journal/Vol01_Issue01/17_Sayoud.pdf

[3] BBC, *'Oldest' Koran fragments found in Birmingham University*, 22 July, 2015 https://www.bbc.com/news/business-33436021

[4] Alba Fedeli, *Collective Enthusiasm And The Cautious Scholar - The Birmingham Quran*, The Marginalia Review of Books, August, 2018 https://marginalia.lareviewofbooks.org/collective-enthusiasm/

Jonathan A. C. Brown, *How should rationalists deal with dogmatism? – The Case of the Birmingham Quran Pages*, Dr. Jonathan Brown, September, 2015 http://drjonathanbrown.com/2015/how-should-rationalists-deal-with-dogmatism-the-case-of-the-birmingham-quran-pages/

[5] Joseph Hoffmann, *The Textual Debacle of the Birmingham Quran*, CrethiPlethi.com, July, 2015 http://www.crethiplethi.com/the-textual-debacle-of-the-birmingham-quran/global-islam/2015/

[6] Gabriel Said Reynolds, *The Birmingham Quran in the context of debate on Islamic origins*, The Times Literary Supplement, 2015 https://www.the-tls.co.uk/articles/variant-readings/

Wesley Huff, *The Birmingham Quran Folios and a Brief Synopsis of its Impact on Islam* https://www.academia.edu/22160060/The_Birmingham_Quran_Folios_and_a_Brief_Synopsis_of_its_Impact_on_Islam

[7] Alba Fedeli, *Collective Enthusiasm And The Cautious Scholar - The Birmingham Quran*, The Marginalia Review of Books, August, 2018 https://marginalia.lareviewofbooks.org/collective-enthusiasm/

[8] Birmingham University, *The Birmingham Quran, Research and conservation* https://www.birmingham.ac.uk/facilities/cadbury/birmingham-quran-mingana-collection/birmingham-quran/research-and-conservation.aspx

[9] Yasin Dutton, *Two 'Hijazi' Fragments of the Quran and their Variants*, Journal of Islamic Manuscripts 8 (2017) 1–56, p45

[10] Anam Rizvi, *A chance to discover the secrets of the Birmingham Quran*, The National, 2017 https://www.thenational.ae/arts-culture/a-chance-to-discover-the-secrets-of-the-birmingham-quran-1.675244

[11] Rich Swier, *How Should We Respond to the Birmingham Quranic Folios*, July, 2015 https://drrichswier.com/2015/07/25/how-should-we-respond-to-the-birmingham-quranic-folios/

Zuher Hassan, *Birmingham Quran Manuscript – Is It As Early As Claimed?* The Muslim News, 2015 http://muslimnews.co.uk/newspaper/comment/birmingham-quran-manuscript-is-it-authentic

Saudi scholars discredit UK's claim of 'oldest Quran', Arabian Business, July, 2015 https://www.arabianbusiness.com/saudi-scholars-discredit-uk-s-claim-of-oldest-quran--600640.html

[12] Alba Fedeli, *Collective Enthusiasm And The Cautious Scholar - The Birmingham Quran*, The Marginalia Review of Books, August, 2018 https://marginalia.lareviewofbooks.org/collective-enthusiasm/

Chapter 17 – Radiocarbon Dating

[1] Greig Watson, *Dating dispute over 'oldest Koran'*, BBC News, 2016 https://www.bbc.com/news/uk-england-35495035

Mike Mcrae, *A Crucial Archaeological Dating Tool Is Wrong, And It Could Change History as We Know It*, ScienceAlert, 2018 https://www.sciencealert.com/radiocarbon-dating-ancient-levant-region-calibration-inaccuracies

Wikipedia, *Radiocarbon dating* https://en.wikipedia.org/wiki/Radiocarbon_dating

[2] François Déroche, *Qurans of the Umayyads: A First Overview*, Brill (2013), p12

[3] Nicolai Sinai, *The Quran: A Historical-Critical Introduction*, Edinburgh University Press, 2017, p46

Nicolai Sinai, *Chapter 1 - The Quran*, in Routledge Handbook on Early Islam, Routledge, 2017, L686

Behnam Sadeghi and Uwe Bergmann, *The codex of the companion of the Prophet and the Quran of the Prophet*, Arabica 57 (2010), pp348-354

[4] Sturt W. Manning, inter alia, *Fluctuating Radiocarbon Offsets Observed in the Southern Levant and Implications for Archaeological Chronology Debates*, Proceedings of the National Academy of Sciences, 2018 https://www.pnas.org/content/115/24/6141

Daniel Aloi, *New radiocarbon cycle research may alter history*, Cornell Chronicle, June, 2018 https://news.cornell.edu/stories/2018/06/new-radiocarbon-cycle-research-may-alter-history

[5] Eva Mira Youssef-Grob, *Radiocarbon (14C) Dating of Early Islamic Documents: Background and Prospects* in *Quran Quotations Preserved on Papyrus Documents, 7th-10th Centuries (Documenta Coranica)*, Brill, 2018

Chapter 18 – Other Manuscript Research

[1] Keith E. Small, *Textual Criticism and Quran Manuscripts*, Lexington, 2011

[2] François Déroche, *Qurans of the Umayyads: A First Overview*, Brill, 2013

[3] Yasin Dutton, Review of *Qurans of the Umayyads: A First Overview by François Déroche*, Journal of Quranic Studies, 18:1 (2016):153–157

[4] Daniel Alan Brubaker, *Corrections in Early Quran Manuscripts: Twenty Examples*, Think and Tell, 2019

[5] Marijn van Putten, *"The Grace of God" as evidence for a written Uthmanic archetype: the importance of shared orthographic idiosyncrasies*, Bulletin of the School of Oriental and African Studies, 82, 2 (2019), pp271–288

[6] Michael Cook, *The Stemma of the Regional Codices of the Koran*, Graeco-Arabica, 9-10 (2004), pp89-104

[7] Behnam Sadeghi and Uwe Bergmann, *The codex of the companion of the Prophet and the Quran of the Prophet*, Arabica 57 (2010), pp367-370

Yasin Dutton, *An Early Mushaf According to the Reading of Ibn Amir*, Journal of Quranic Studies, 3/1 (2001), pp71-89

Yasin Dutton, *Some Notes on the British Library's 'Oldest Quran Manuscript'* (Or. 2165), Journal of Quranic Studies, 6 (2004), pp43-71

Marijn van Putten, *Hisham's Ibraham: Evidence for a Canonical Quranic Reading Based on the Rasm*, Journal of the Royal Asiatic Society, Vol. 30, Issue 2 (2020), pp231-250

Bibliography

A B

Altikulaç, Tayyar. *Al-Mushaf al-Sharif attributed to Uthman bin Affan*, Research Centre For Islamic History, Art and Culture (IRCICA), 2007

Anthony, Sean W. *Two 'Lost' Suras of the Quran: Surat al-Khal and Surat al-Hafd between Textual and Ritual Canon*, JSAI 46, 2019

al-Azami, Muhammad Mustafa. *The History of the Quranic Text from Revelation to Compilation*, UK Islamic Academy, 2003

Bellamy, James A. *Textual Criticism of the Quran*, in Encyclopaedia of the Quran, Brill

Berg, Herbert. *Routledge Handbook on Early Islam*, Routledge, 2017

----. *Collection and Canonization of the Quran*, in *Routledge Handbook on Early Islam*, Routledge, 2017

----. *The Devine Sources*, in *The Ashgate Research Companion to Islamic Law*, Ashgate, 2014

----. *Context: Muhammad*, in *Wiley Blackwell Companion to the Quran*, Wiley-Blackwell, 2006, 2017

Birmingham University, The Birmingham Quran
https://www.birmingham.ac.uk/facilities/cadbury/birmingham-quran-mingana-collection/birmingham-quran/index.aspx

----. The Birmingham Quran, Research and conservation
https://www.birmingham.ac.uk/facilities/cadbury/birmingham-quran-mingana-collection/birmingham-quran/research-and-conservation.aspx

Boekhoff-van der Voort, Nicolet. *Between History and Legend: The Biography of the Prophet Muhammad by Ibn Shihab al-Zuhri*. PhD thesis, 2012. To be published

Brown, Jonathan A. C. *Hadith (The Foundations of Islam)*, Oneworld Publications, 2017

----. *How should rationalists deal with dogmatism? – The Case of the Birmingham Quran Pages*, September 2015
http://drjonathanbrown.com/2015/how-should-rationalists-deal-with-dogmatism-the-case-of-the-birmingham-quran-pages/

Brubaker, Daniel Alan. *Corrections in Early Quran Manuscripts: Twenty Examples*, Think and Tell, 2019

Bursi, Adam. *Connecting the Dots: Diacritics, Scribal Culture, and the Quran in the First/Seventh Century*, Journal of the International Quranic Studies Association, Vol. 3 (2018), pp111-157

Burton, John. *The Collection of the Quran*, Cambridge University Press, 1977

C D E F

Cellard, Eleonore. Review of *The Sanaa Palimpsest: The Transmission of the Quran in the First Centuries AH* by Asma Hilali, Review of Quranic Research, Vol. 5, no. 9, 2019

Cook, Michael. *Muhammad (Past Masters)*, Oxford University Press, 1983, 1999

Corpus Coranicum Project. Project Goals
https://corpuscoranicum.de/
https://corpuscoranicum.de/about/index/sure/1/vers/1

Denny, Frederick M. *Exegesis and recitation: their development as classical forms of Quranic piety*, in *Transitions and Transformations in the History of Religions: Essays in Honor of Joseph M. Kitagawa*, Brill, 1980

Déroche, François. *Qurans of the Umayyads: A First Overview*, Brill, 2013

----. *Written Transmission*, in *Wiley Blackwell Companion to the Quran*, Wiley-Blackwell, 2017

Donner, Fred M. *The Quran In Recent Scholarship,* in *The Quran in its Historical Context,* Routledge, 2008

----. *Narratives of Islamic Origins: The Beginnings of Islamic Historical Writing,* Darwin Press, 1998

----. *The Study of Islams Origins Since W. Montgomery Watt's Publications,* Paper presented November 2015, at the University of Edinburgh https://www.scribd.com/document/360940402/The-Study-of-Islams-Origins-Since-W-Montgomery-Watt-s-Publications

----. Review of Textual Criticism and Quran Manuscripts, by Keith E. Small, Journal of Near Eastern Studies 73, no. 1, April 2014

Dutton, Yasin, *Orality, Literacy and the Seven Ahruf Hadith,* Journal of Islamic Studies 23:1 (2012) pp1–49

----. *Two 'Hijazi' Fragments of the Quran and their Variants,* Journal of Islamic Manuscripts 8, 2017

----. Review of *Qurans of the Umayyads: A First Overview* by François Déroche. Journal of Quranic Studies 18:1, 2016

Fedeli, Alba. *Early Evidences of Variant Readings in Quranic Manuscripts,* in *The Hidden Origins of Islam: New Research into Its Early History,* Prometheus Books, 2008

----. *Collective Enthusiasm And The Cautious Scholar - The Birmingham Quran,* The Marginalia Review of Books, August, 2018 https://marginalia.lareviewofbooks.org/collective-enthusiasm/

G H I J K

Gilchrist, John. *The Codification of the Quran Text,* Answering Islam, 1989 https://www.answering-islam.org/Gilchrist/Jam/index.html

Gilliot, Claude. *Creation of a Fixed Text* in *The Cambridge Companion to the Quran,* Cambridge University Press, 2006

Green, Samuel. *The Preservation Of The Quran - An Examination Of The Common Claims Made About The Quran*, 2017
https://www.answering-islam.org/Green/uthman.htm

Hamdan, Omar. *The Second Masahif Project: A Step Towards the Canonization of the Quranic Text*, in *The Quran in Context: Historical and Literary Investigations Into the Quranic Milieu*, Brill Academic Publishers, 2009

Hassan, Zuher. *Birmingham Quran Manuscript – Is It As Early As Claimed?* The Muslim News, 2015
http://muslimnews.co.uk/newspaper/comment/birmingham-quran-manuscript-is-it-authentic

Hilali, Asma. *The Sanaa Palimpsest: The Transmission of the Quran in the First Centuries AH.*, OUP/Institute of Ismaili Studies, 2017

Islamic Awareness, *Codex Sanaa 1 – A Quranic Manuscript From Mid–1st Century Of Hijra - History Of The Manuscript*
https://www.islamic-awareness.org/quran/text/mss/soth

Jeffery, Arthur. *Materials for the History of the Text of the Quran: The Old Codices*, E.J. Brill, 1937

Jones, A. *The History of the Text of the Quran after the Death of Muhammad*, in *The Quran II*, in *Arabic Literature to the End of the Umayyad Period*, Cambridge University Press, 1983, 2010

----. *The Quran in Muhammad's Lifetime*, in *The Quran II*, in *Arabic Literature to the End of the Umayyad Period*, Cambridge University Press, 1983, 2010

Kaplony, Andreas. Michael Marx. *Quran Quotations Preserved on Papyrus Documents, 7th-10th Centuries (Documenta Coranica)*, Brill, 2018

Khatib, Ammar. Nazir Khan. *The Origins of the Variant Readings of the Quran*, Yaqeen Institute for Islamic Research, 2020
https://yaqeeninstitute.org/ammar-khatib/the-origins-of-the-variant-readings-of-the-quran

L M N O P

Lalani, Arzina R. *Ali b. Abi Talib*, in *The Quran: An Encyclopedia*, Routledge, 2005

Leemhuis, Frederik. *Readings of the Quran*, in *Encyclopaedia of the Quran*, Brill

Mcrae, Mike. *A Crucial Archaeological Dating Tool Is Wrong, And It Could Change History as We Know It*, ScienceAlert, 2018
https://www.sciencealert.com/radiocarbon-dating-ancient-levant-region-calibration-inaccuracies

Melchert, Christopher. *Ibn Mujahid and the Establishment of the Seven Quranic Readings*, Studia Islamica, 2000, no. 91

----. *The Relation of the Ten Readings to One Another*, Journal of
    Quranic Studies, 2008, no. 10

Modarressi, Hossein. *Early Debates on the Integrity of the Quran: A Brief Survey*, Studia Islamica, No. 77, 1993

Motzki, Harold. *Alternative Accounts of the Quran's Formation*, in *The Cambridge Companion to the Quran*, Cambridge University Press, 2006

----. *Hadith: Origins and Developments*, Routledge, 2004, 2016

----. *The Collection of the Quran A Reconsideration of Western Views in
    Light of Recent Methodological Developments*, Der Islam, Vol. 78,
    Issue 1, pp1-34, 2001

Watt, W. Montgomery. Richard L. Bell. *Introduction to the Quran*, Edinburgh University Press, 1970, 1995

Neuwirth, Angelika. *Structure And Emergence Of Community*, in *Wiley Blackwell Companion to the Quran*, Wiley-Blackwell, 2006, 2017

Nöldeke, Theodor. Friedrich Schwally, Gotthelf Bergsträsser, Otto Pretzl, *The History of the Quran*, Brill, 1937

Paton, Alan. *Hadith: What, Why, and When....*, Parkhill Books, 2018

Powers, David S. *Muhammad Is Not the Father of Any of Your Men: The Making of the Last Prophet*, University of Pennsylvania Press, 2009

----. *Zayd (Divinations: Rereading Late Ancient Religion)*, University of Pennsylvania Press, 2014

----. *Sinless, Sonless and Seal of Prophets: Muhammad and Quran 33, 36-40, Revisited*, Arabica 67:4 (2020)

van Putten, Marijn. *"The Grace of God" as evidence for a written Uthmanic archetype: the importance of shared orthographic idiosyncrasies*, Bulletin of the School of Oriental and African Studies, 82, 2 (2019), pp271–288

----. *Hisham's Ibraham: Evidence for a Canonical Quranic Reading Based on the Rasm*, Journal of the Royal Asiatic Society, Vol. 30, Issue 2 (2020), pp231-250

R S

Reynolds, Gabriel Said. *The Emergence of Islam: Classical Traditions in Contemporary Perspective*, Fortress Press, 2012

----. *New Perspectives on the Quran: The Quran in its Historical Context 2*, Routledge, 2011, 2014

----. *Introduction: Quranic Studies and its Controversies*, in *The Quran in its Historical Context*, Routledge, 2007

Robinson, Chase F. *Abd al-Malik (Makers of the Muslim World)*, Oneworld Publications, 2005

----. *Islamic Historiography*, Cambridge University Press, 2003

Robinson, Neal. *Discovering the Quran: A Contemporary Approach to a Veiled Text*, Georgetown University Press, 1996, 2004

Sadeghi, Behnam. Mohsen Goudarzi, *Sanaa 1 and the Origins of the Quran*, Der Islam 87 (2012)

Sadeghi, Behnam. Uwe Bergmann, *The codex of the companion of the Prophet and the Quran of the Prophet*, Arabica 57 (2010)

Sadeghi, Behnam. *Origins of the Koran: From revelation to holy book*, BBC, 2015 https://www.bbc.co.uk/news/world-middle-east-33631745

Sayoud, Halim. *Statistical Analysis of the Birmingham Quran Folios*, HDSKD journal, Vol. 4, No. 1, 2018 http://scholarpage.org/journal/Vol01_Issue01/17_Sayoud.pdf

Schoeler, Gregor. *The Codification of the Quran: A Comment on the Hypotheses of Burton and Wansbrough* in *The Quran in Context: Historical and Literary Investigations Into the Quranic Milieu*, Brill Academic Publishers, 2009

Sfar, Mondher. *In Search of the Original Koran: The True History of the Revealed Text*, Prometheus Books, 2008

Shoemaker, Stephen J. *The Death of a Prophet: The End of Muhammad's Life and the Beginnings of Islam*, University of Pennsylvania Press, 2011

----. *Muhammad And The Quran*, in *The Oxford Handbook of Late Antiquity*, OUP USA, 2012

Sinai, Nicolai. *Beyond the Cairo Edition: On the Study of Early Quranic Codices*, Journal of the American Oriental Society 140.1 (2020)

----. *The Quran: A Historical-Critical Introduction*, Edinburgh University Press, 2017

----. *Chapter 1 - The Quran*, in *Routledge Handbook on Early Islam*, Routledge, 2017

----. *When did the consonantal skeleton of the Quran reach closure?* Bulletin of the School of Oriental and African Studies 77, 2014

Small, Keith E. *Textual Criticism and Quran Manuscripts*, Lexington, 2011

Stewart, Devin. Gabriel Said Reynolds. *Afterword: The Academic Study of the Quran - Achievements, Challenges, and Prospects*, JIQSA 1, 2016

T U V W X Y Z

Tesei, Tommaso. *'The Romans Will Win!' Q 30:2–7 in Light of 7th C. Political Eschatology*, Der Islam 2018, 95 (1)

Thompson, Keith. *Lost and forgotten Parts of the Koran*, in *The Corruption of the Koran: Evidence and New Research*, Exegetical Apologetics, 2018
http://www.exegeticalapologetics.com/2018/05/the-corruption-of-koran-evidence-and.html

Turner, Steven. *A review and investigation of 8th century Christian polemics against the Quran*, Arabic 5701, 2017

Wansbrough, John. *Quranic Studies: Sources and Methods of Scriptural Interpretation*, Prometheus Books, 1977, 2004

----. *Sectarian Milieu: Content and Composition of Islamic Salvation History*, Prometheus Books, 1978, 2006

Wayne, Luke. *Have there been changes to the Quran?* 2016
https://carm.org/have-there-been-changes-in-the-quran

Welch, Alford T. *History of the Quran after 632*, in *The Quran*, in *Encyclopaedia of Islam*, Second Edition, Brill

Whelan, Estelle. *Forgotten Witness: Evidence For The Early Codification Of The Quran*, Journal of The American Oriental Society, 1998, Vol. 118

WikiIslam, the online resource on Islam,
https://wikiislam.net/wiki/Corruption_of_the_Quran

Wikipedia, Sanaa manuscript
https://en.wikipedia.org/wiki/Sanaa_manuscript

----. Birmingham Quran manuscript
https://en.wikipedia.org/wiki/Birmingham_Quran_manuscript

White, James. *What Every Christian Needs to Know About the Quran*, Bethany House, 2013

Youssef-Grob, Eva Mira. *Radiocarbon (14C) Dating of Early Islamic Documents: Background and Prospects* in *Quran Quotations Preserved on Papyrus Documents, 7th-10th Centuries (Documenta Coranica)*, Brill, 2018

Zayd, Nasr Abu. *Towards Understanding the Quran's Worldview*, in *New Perspectives on the Quran: The Quran in its Historical Context 2*, Routledge, 2011, 2014